Focused Lesson Planning

Focused Lesson Planning

Helping Teachers Examine and Develop Their Own Mindset

Urban Fraefel

ROWMAN & LITTLEFIELD
Lanham • Boulder • New York • London

Published by Rowman & Littlefield
An imprint of The Rowman & Littlefield Publishing Group, Inc.
4501 Forbes Boulevard, Suite 200, Lanham, Maryland 20706
www.rowman.com

86-90 Paul Street, London EC2A 4NE

British Library Cataloguing in Publication Information Available

Library of Congress Cataloging-in-Publication Data

Names: Fraefel, Urban, 1953- author.
Title: Focused lesson planning : helping teachers examine and develop their own mindset / Urban Fraefel.
Description: Lanham : Rowman & Littlefield, [2023] | Includes bibliographical references. | Summary: "This book shows teachers how to plan units and lessons in a highly focused and effective way that is lean, timesaving, professional, and free of unnecessary trivialities"-- Provided by publisher.
Identifiers: LCCN 2023009447 (print) | LCCN 2023009448 (ebook) | ISBN 9781475869095 (cloth) | ISBN 9781475869101 (paperback) | ISBN 9781475869118 (ebook)
Subjects: LCSH: Lesson planning. | Teacher effectiveness. | Educational evaluation.
Classification: LCC LB1027.4 .F73 2023 (print) | LCC LB1027.4 (ebook) | DDC 371.3028--dc23/eng/20230407
LC record available at https://lccn.loc.gov/2023009447
LC ebook record available at https://lccn.loc.gov/2023009448

♾™ The paper used in this publication meets the minimum requirements of American National Standard for Information Sciences—Permanence of Paper for Printed Library Materials, ANSI/NISO Z39.48-1992.

Contents

Foreword

Frank Lyman

Planning in education and teacher education is often a rudderless enterprise. As soon as the prospective teachers begin student teaching and then full-time classroom teaching, they tend to plan their strategy and the activities without sufficient attention to goals, motivation, student buy-in, assessment, sequence, or what they know about learning theory. The reasons are several, but central is the fact that planning takes time and teachers don't feel like they can spare it. This book convincingly examines the reasons for the disconnect between what is known about effective planning for teaching and the actual implementation of the same in preservice teacher education.

The author makes clear that teachers require a mindset for planning. This mindset must include placing the students' needs, abilities, knowledge, and point of view at the center of the lesson or unit plan and enabling students to be involved, understand, practice, apply, and transfer their learning.

The author sets forth a thorough discussion and description of the backward planning model. This model begins with establishing a clear vision of what students will learn or be able to do, then what tasks they will have to perform to do it. The tasks they perform are tightly tied to the understood goals of the lesson or unit. Once it is clear what the students will do, the teacher can plot the course of the lesson.

Crucial with this approach is that students have an understanding of where they are headed and why what they are doing is important. The students' point of view is always kept in mind. Motivation is essential and more likely when students are involved in the goal-setting process. Thus, the heart of the planning process is the students' willingness to learn what they believe to be important.

Although this approach—planning backward from a joint endeavor of goal setting, to establishing clarity about how learning will be assessed, to the strategy for teaching—seems reasonable, too frequently it is not adopted within the situational press of the classroom.

Moreover, as the author explains, it is too rarely adopted within the student teaching experience. The importance of this book on planning is the thorough detailing of all aspects of backward planning such that coaches in field-based programs can demonstrate to student teachers that planning is not a time-stealing process, but rather a way to centralize student involvement and to know to what extent their teaching has been successful.

From my experience over twenty-six years with more than one thousand K–12 student teachers as a university field supervisor, I can attest that planning was usually left to chance. The result of this was that the focus was less on the primacy of student buy-in and performance than it was on strategy and how smoothly the lesson ran. Though the maximum-student-response strategies were effective, the opportunity to turn the learning process over to the students was diminished.

This detailed exposition of placing all dimensions of student-understood goals, tasks, and assessment in the forefront is a great contribution to the beginning stages of teacher education. It lays out a way forward to tie the campus and field experiences together. No teacher educator who takes the author's concern and remedy seriously will neglect planning as a central aspect of student teaching. The book would have rounded out the edges of this former teacher educator's program.

Frank Lyman, PhD, is a teacher educator and educational consultant. He is along with Arlene Mindus the originator of think-pair-share, arguably the most used every-student-response, cooperative discussion design at all educational levels in the United States and abroad.

Preface

Teachers spend, on average, about one-fifth of their total work time planning and preparing lessons. If teachers invest so much time, it should be used rationally, purposefully, and promisingly. Therefore, widespread habits of planning should be questioned and, if necessary, improved.

Asking around teachers, one becomes aware of a huge range of opinions on planning and starts to wonder: Is a quick fill-in-the-blank template enough? Should one simply follow scripted lessons or textbooks and forgo planning? To what extent does one need to study standards and curricula? Should one tailor planning to individual students? Or is the purpose of planning primarily to make the lesson run smoothly?

This book clearly points in one direction: it puts student learning first, and planning must be aligned with that goal. Therefore, everything that is commonly done in planning should be examined to see if it ultimately serves the progress and well-being of the students. Anything that does not contribute to this goal must be radically questioned.

However, this book also considers the needs of teachers. It is not uncommon, especially in teacher education, to find excessive, time-consuming, and often useless planning rituals. But planning can in fact be highly professional and at the same time lean and focused.

Planning is a core practice of every teacher, as are many other core practices that need to be understood, adapted to the situation at hand, and applied effectively. In terms of the basic principles of planning, therefore, this book is aimed at all teachers at every level and in every subject; domain- and level-specific issues are addressed only in passing.

A Workbook

The intent is not merely to inform about planning, but to help teachers actually improve it. Therefore, as the author, I do not take a neutral position, but rather take sides in favor of planning procedures that best help students to make progress and that help teachers to create lean, efficient, and resource-saving plans. The structure of this book is designed to serve this goal and is characterized by the following features:

- **Spiral principle:** Some topics are addressed multiple times throughout the book, and each time, new aspects are added, or the topic is explored further. For example, the important but not simple topic of goal setting comes up again and again, allowing the reader to gradually understand it better.
- **Further information and resources:** The reader will repeatedly encounter boxes with this title. These are more in-depth sections that supplement the continuous text, can also be skipped over as the book is read through, and can be studied in more detail according to need or interest.
- **Activities and suggestions:** The boxes headed with this title are primarily intended for teachers or student teachers who want to work through the book themselves and learn the practices of focused planning. Quite specific and detailed tasks are provided that can be used to better understand the topics covered in each chapter and to practice procedures. However, these boxes can also provide ideas for teacher educators and cooperating teachers working with student teachers.

1

⚭

The Approach in Brief

WHY EFFECTIVE PLANNING SHOULD BE FOCUSED AND LEAN

Let's face it: planning is a rather stressful subject, and teachers enjoy teaching more than planning. Planning and preparing lessons is undeniably important, but it's just what needs to be done before the real thing, that is, before teaching. Planning steals time that we would rather spend on working with children and young people.

In addition, we face an irritating problem: there is no consensus on what constitutes good planning. Expectations on how to carry out planning are extremely divergent: especially in teacher education, the demands on planning are high; planning is supposed to draw on the broad knowledge of the subject and pedagogy, and this knowledge is supposed to be translated in a virtual way into practical work when planning—a very difficult undertaking for prospective teachers with little experience.

On the other hand, it is very important to in-service teachers that planning be simple, quick, purposeful, and efficient, because they do not have time to make complicated planning considerations and come up with sophisticated lesson concepts.

To put it somewhat succinctly in a nutshell: in teacher education, planning is (over)complicated; in schools, it is (over)simplified.

One wonders: How can it be that in the teaching profession, many of the recommendations made by experts in education are so far removed from what practitioners actually do? After all, in most professions, what the experts expect and what the practitioners do converge over time; the practitioners increasingly learn what is "state of the art," and the experts

1

learn from the practitioners how the day-to-day operations of the profession work. Pros in most professions—doctors, builders, technicians, pilots, accountants, foresters, and many more—take pride in doing things the way the experts in their training think they should.

Not so much with teachers. A great many teachers set aside the demanding planning routines of teacher education as soon as they enter the profession, seeking simpler procedures, prefabricated lessons, clear lesson planning templates, and time-saving concepts. Teachers often find themselves in this dilemma: either elaborate, thoughtful planning that is well grounded in subject matter and pedagogy, or more minimalist procedures that plan primarily for lesson management, secretly knowing that they should actually be planning more thoroughly.

Clearly, then, the teaching profession is living with inconsistencies when it comes to planning. This is troubling in a profession as important as teaching. There would need to be a way to make the planning issue coherent so that both the professional demands are satisfied and the needs and expectations of teachers in the profession are met. What is the solution?

Let's keep in mind what the most straightforward starting point is: Teachers are supposed to plan lessons in a way that will help students progress. Planning must focus on instruction that promotes learning. Planning can therefore never just mean structuring and preparing a lesson, but planning must mean ensuring the learning success of the students. Furthermore, planning must be focused, lean, simple, and purposeful because teachers want to use their limited time to plan as effectively as possible.

The Basic Planning Concept: What Do Students Need to Do?

The many questions and ideas surrounding planning can basically be reduced to one: What do students need to do so that they can learn? When this question is consistently at the center, planning becomes much easier. The essential takes place with the students: Is listening enough? Should they write? Solve tasks, and if so, which ones? Am I sure that they will learn something by doing so, or do they need more? Should they discuss, should they develop ideas and express themselves, should they practice drill? Should they test themselves? So, it's always about what the students are doing to get ahead and preventing them from falling by the wayside.

This approach takes pressure off the teachers, who don't constantly have to worry about what they need to do. The main actor is not the teacher, but the students. The engine of learning, so to speak, is in the students; the teacher only needs to activate it. The teacher's job is interpreted in a humbler way: helping students make progress.

Three Steps, Starting with Where Students Should Stand at the End

This book proposes a consistent simplification of the planning process. This is to make planning professional, effective, and lean at the same time. It requires mainly three steps:

1. A preparatory step: a clear *vision of where students should be at the end*, that is, the teacher envisions as precisely as possible what students will be able to do, know, accomplish, decide, answer, produce, and so forth at the end (actually, these are the goals, even if we have not yet named them as such). In other words, the teacher is envisioning the *desired outcomes*. This step is tightly coupled with the next one.
2. The core step: the teacher fleshes out this vision (these goals) in *specific tasks*; therefore, whoever masters these tasks has achieved the goals. These tasks are for assessment as well as learning—there should be no difference. Either way, they represent exactly what the goal of the lesson is. So, the tasks have to be designed in such a way that they can be used to learn and test exactly what corresponds to the vision.

These two steps are closely linked and belong together inseparably. Without the vision of where the journey is going, all activities and tasks are aimless in the strictest sense of the word, and conversely, visions—goals—are without any impact if one does not know with which activities and tasks they are to be achieved and the achievement is to be tested.

Designing the lesson plan will follow only at the end, which takes a little getting used to:

3. The final, organizational step is to *anticipate the course of the lesson*—something that many teachers consider far too important, but which actually follows quite logically from the previous steps.

This approach of "backward planning" is not new, but it goes against the intuition of many teachers who know forward planning and first ask themselves what the *teacher* should do in the lesson (set the course of the lesson, explain, ask questions, organize, test, etc.) and only afterward might ask themselves what the students have to do, how they will learn, and how the progress will be checked. In our approach of backward planning, however, the practicalities of the lesson plan are not neglected, but they are taken up only in a final step, as they are largely derived from more important points to be clarified beforehand (see figure 1.1).

Clearly, teachers want some certainty about how lessons will go, and that is understandable. They do not want the flow of the lesson to fail. Yet

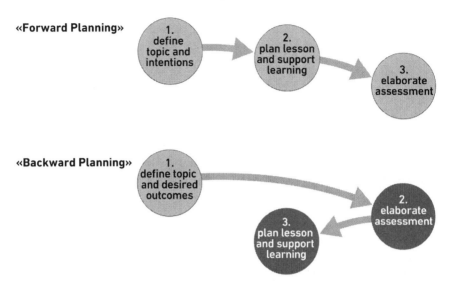

Figure 1.1.   Two principles of the planning process: forward and backward planning. *Created by the author*

they are more likely to get that certainty if they plan from the students' point of view and don't think so much about themselves first. The really important thing is to ensure student learning, that is, that they immerse themselves in it, are involved in it, can do it, understand it, practice it, apply it, transfer it. That's what planning is going to be about. So, planning will provide a very solid foundation, free of superficialities, for teaching that is truly conducive to learning.

Backward Planning Will Change Many Habits

Starting from the end (with where the teacher intends the students to stand in the end) has some implications for teaching and planning.

You will see tasks as the linchpin of planning

Basically, everything revolves around tasks. There are always tasks to check the learning progress, whereby, as we know, there is everything from mindless test items to authentic or simulated tasks in which a problem has to be solved or something has to be created. The field of possible tasks is very, very wide; teachers should not hesitate to use the full range of possible task types to support all students' abilities. More on that later. For learning progress, there needs to be tasks, activities, problems, which the students gradually learn to master.

And another thing: the tasks are full of content and goals, both inherent in the tasks, *if* the tasks are set well and coherently. One could say: show me your tasks and I will tell you what the goals and contents of your lessons *really* are.

You will be more transparent and willing to engage in dialogue

It's not enough for only the teacher to know where the journey is headed. This approach requires full transparency to everything the teacher has thought about and planned. Students need to know what is expected of them at the end, and they may want to offer comments, concerns, and suggestions. It is reasonable that students often have their say in what, how, and in what time they are to learn.

The goals should be set and communicated in a way that students can truly understand and make their own. They need to know what they are doing it for, and to what extent they are making progress or still having difficulties; they should also know exactly how their progress will be checked at the end. So, get comfortable with the idea that you will disclose all tasks and test items along with the success criteria and solutions at any time.

Besides, students' eagerness to meet goals is not a given. Therefore, a successful teacher will not ignore the voice of students. This requires a great openness to dialogue on the part of the teacher, because if everyone is to be on the same page to achieve the goals, there needs to be understanding and discussion rather than imposition. We know that pressure, fear, and dodging discomfort are poor ways to get students to achieve more; rather, a partnership approach is needed.

You will see formative learning support as your key activity on the path to learning success

The heart of a lesson is not the teacher's performance, but the students' activity. Everything the teacher does serves to energize that core. If teachers truly understand teaching as a joint endeavor with students, they will do their part to ensure that all students can take their steps. In the case of grit in the gears, the teacher will then seek ways to have difficulties of all kinds dealt with.

You will dive deeper than ever into student tasks and understand them in any way possible

Teachers should themselves understand the tasks they give students. This is actually so self-evident that it hardly needs to be said; and yet, teachers themselves do not always really understand in depth what they expect from students, especially if they have not constructed tasks themselves and hastily gather them from numerous sources.

For the teacher, dealing with the tasks thoroughly means (1) understanding and mastering the content addressed in the task precisely and from many perspectives, and (2) also seeing the tasks from the point of view of the students, who may have difficulties with them or develop unorthodox approaches. Both—understanding the content and experiencing the student's perspective—are indispensable prerequisites for supporting students in their learning.

2

⊗

The Primacy of Impact and the Wisdom of Practitioners

School and teaching are there to have an impact. It is not for nothing that communities, government agencies, families, organizations of all kinds, and, of course, teachers and other staff spend enormous amounts of resources to educate the next generation and introduce them to the workings of our society. All this effort only makes sense if something results from it. Up to this point, everyone probably agrees.

Now, if it is the teachers' duty to create an impact, one may assume that they invest all their energy in this duty and focus the instruction on making sure that the students progress on their way. Again, that seems to be indisputable. But the reality—particularly with less experienced teachers and with student teachers—is often different. This can be seen especially in the strategies of planning.

All who make a plan do so to accomplish something. This is true in all professions and occupations, and in the private sphere as well. For example, you want to get to a certain place, you want to finish a product, you want to start a business, you want to win a game—when you make a plan, it is always aimed at achieving success. But what about lesson planning? Is success really always the goal of the plan?

WHAT'S THE POINT OF PLANNING?
THREE COMMON OPTIONS

Let's take a step back and look at what teachers actually plan for, what they expect from planning. Roughly speaking, we know of three types of planning in the reality of teaching and teacher education, which we briefly describe here. Simply by describing them, it becomes obvious which types are really aimed at having an impact on learners and which are not.

Option 1: Does the Planning Primarily Aim at Having a Lesson Plan?

Very often, the product of a planning is understood as a *document* that you can hold in your hands (lesson plan, lesson outline). For this purpose, countless instructions circulate, often divided into a general part on goals and content, followed by a chronological sequencing for the phases. The size is sometimes even interpreted as a sign of quality. This "planning" sometimes turns out to be an artifact of teacher education, an often highly elaborated product according to the specifications of the institution or the professional staff of teacher education but is hardly ever used in this form in everyday professional life.

As Arkansas teacher educators note in a study on planning: "It is not uncommon among teachers in our geographical area to find public school teachers who are writing ten to fifteen pages of lesson plans to document the classroom instruction of one single day. That is a tremendous amount of writing. Can we blame our public school colleagues for getting weary of their profession if those are the demands?" (Womack et al., 2015).

Option 2: Must Planning Mainly Ensure a Successfully Running Lesson?

The purpose of planning can also be understood as a successfully running lesson that takes place as planned (in which case a failed lesson would be one in which the teacher cannot carry out the planned steps). The actual lesson is, in a way, the materialization of the reflections that the student teacher or teacher has made. The focus here is on the teacher's *performance*.

There are good reasons to contradict: in school, a well-planned lesson that goes as intended is not the goal, but at best a means to an end. In professional practice, teachers do not need to deliver teaching as if it were a product. It is not a matter of arranging the available time according to certain rules. Teaching does not have to be sophisticated; it is not a work of art, not a creative self-realization of the teacher. And the fact that the lesson plan is worked out in detail is not likely to interest the students very much.

It is true that the teacher's primary concern is to design this very lesson, but the visible staging would have to serve a purpose; the functioning of the plan is not enough when it comes to learning success. The course of the lesson is merely a framework in which the essential things—learning, understanding, insight, interest, progress, ability, cooperation, competence—can take place. If the essential does not occur, only an empty shell remains, no matter how pleasingly and smoothly everything proceeds. Artfully twisted teaching is a pseudoproblem: students don't need "variety," creative and original ideas just for the sake of it. Rather, they want to understand what it is all about, what they have to do, and how to achieve it, and this in an appreciative atmosphere.

Option 3: Will a Good Plan Manifest Itself in the Progress of the Students?

In extracurricular contexts, a plan is associated with a firm intention to achieve something, to *succeed* in something. In a school context, it cannot seriously be called a "success" if the planned lessons run smoothly. It is about much more: according to the educational mission, the desirable outcome of a plan can only be that students make progress—in cognitive, physical, social, aesthetic, creative, motivational, and emotional areas. Conversely, if students leave a lesson in which nothing "happened," that is, nothing moved on any level or they did not learn or consolidate or better understand anything, then one rightly wonders what all the effort was for.

Which Options Are Preferable?

Certainly, each of the options has its own logic in its context:

- For student teachers who need the approval of teacher educators to complete their studies, option 1 is particularly important.
- Those who want to maintain control, and those who are inexperienced and unsure about organizing instruction, will see help in the second option. A reasonable amount of sequencing is useful for the teacher and the students; there is nothing wrong with that as long as control of the lesson does not become the dominant principle.
- Good teachers are the ones who want to achieve something and whose students learn as well and sustainably as possible, and therefore, they are guided by the third option. It is the only one that takes into account the real purpose of teaching. Thus, option 3 is primarily the manifestation of a responsive mindset.

Of these three interpretations of "planning," *particularly the third option* is the one that student teachers should acquire to be prepared for the real challenges of the profession, while the first two options can be seen as a kind of support in teacher education in which the real professionals have little interest because they are not of much use to them.

YOUR PLANNING DOCUMENTS:
WHAT IS THE CURRENT STATUS?

1. Find at least half a dozen lesson plans that you have put into practice in real life, possibly from different contexts (e.g., practicum, internships, teaching on your own, "model lessons," introductions, phases with primarily learning activities).
2. As described previously, there are three types/options of planning lessons. They are often interwoven in reality, as shown in these four categories:
   i.   Notes written down simply for the sake of not forgetting and getting it all together
   ii.   Parts written down only because it is prescribed to mention them in the lesson plan
   iii. Parts to control the flow of the lesson and keep you from the unexpected, designed to ensure that the lesson does not slip away
   iv.   Parts written down to make room for better understanding and deeper learning, to make student learning as effective as possible, and to support student progress
3. Skim the planning documents and assign each part to one of the four categories above (e.g., using colors). Perhaps the four categories overlap here and there. Do you see any clustering, patterns, or deficiencies?
4. Note in a few words the extent to which you identify problems or need for action regarding your planning practices.

HOW DO EXPERIENCED TEACHERS PLAN?

A study by Hatch and Clark (2021) of expert rural teachers summarizes their planning and decision making this way: "The teachers didn't write elaborate lesson plans or rely heavily on curriculum programs. Instead, teachers utilized teaching strategies, disciplined improvisation, knowledge of their students, learning outcomes, and formal and informal assessment to drive instruction" (p. 1).

This summary is typical of a great many teachers. We know that teachers who have a few years of professional practice under their belt pretty much don't use the templates and procedures prescribed in teacher education. It is interesting to see what procedures experienced teachers adopt instead. It is worth looking at how successful and experienced expert teachers plan their flexible, varied lessons that best support students' individual progress. Studies have been published on this subject repeatedly for many years (e.g., Yinger, 1980; also Wernke & Zierer, 2017; on expert teachers: Berliner, 2001).

Expert teachers seem to have a number of things at their disposal that make it easier for them to plan lessons. Among other things, the following points are characteristic of expert teachers (summarized in Hatch & Clark, 2021; König et al., 2015; Munthe & Conway, 2017; Seel, 1997; Shavelson, 1987):

1. **Knowing where the students stand and monitoring learning progress**—For expert teachers to know how their students are doing and how the whole class is doing, they habitually use all available information: observations, conversations, informal feedback, student work, sometimes tests and surveys for formative purposes.
2. **Knowing what is to be learned: content, skills, competencies, understanding**—Expert teachers focus their content planning on what students actually have to master. They know the standards set by the state and use them as a matter of course, and they use good learning materials, if these are available.
3. **Sharpened intuitions**—They have developed expertise in dealing with decision-making situations: they intuitively "feel" what to do at this moment, how to adjust the course of action, how to solve the problem, what is urgent now, and so forth. The result of such adaptive teaching is what Sawyer (2004) terms "disciplined improvisation."
4. **Developing and using their own routines**—They have numerous everyday routines for which they hardly give a second thought. These help to organize the course of instruction calmly (Kagan, 1992; Yinger, 1980).

Apparently, expert teachers experience these four areas as particularly supportive, without them having to be part of the written and detailed lesson plan. Competencies in the four areas are the foundation on which they plan their lessons. After initial teacher education, these teachers developed their simplified planning routines. These gravitate mainly around *selection and support of tasks and assignments* to be carried out by the students, which corresponds quite well to the situation in real professional life.

If, after a few years, teachers quite pragmatically acquire their own and obviously expedient planning routines—then why not precisely analyze these procedures in order to learn from them in initial teacher education and choose those that are successful and expedient for expert teachers? It still doesn't seem to be all that common in the teaching profession, what is completely self-evident in the vast majority of professions.

In other professions, what is learned in training is mostly what can be used later. In daily work, the knowledge and recommendations can be put together and combined with one's own experience and the needs of the situation. This simple principle of learning from the best and most successful professional people is not new; it also underlies expert research on the teaching profession (Berliner, 2001; Borko & Livingston, 1989).

WHAT CAN WE LEARN FROM EXPERIENCED EXPERT TEACHERS?

So, what does all this mean for planning instruction? The view here is a pragmatic one, that is, "What contributes to the solution of the problem? What helps meet the challenge?" Therefore, the elements that follow are not based primarily on theory, but on plausibility and experience.

No Excessive Analysis of Content, but Deep Understanding of Student Tasks

Absolutely no one disputes that teachers should be knowledgeable about subject matter. However, this is not primarily about academic knowledge, but about the subjects that students have to learn (pedagogical content knowledge [PCK], see box to follow). At this level, teachers should understand the content *in its full depth*. Teachers must be able to flexibly master the subject matter from different perspectives, which unfortunately not all teachers are equally capable of doing (see box "What Is Meant by 'Understanding the Content'?").

Therefore, it is a largely unnecessary effort to reanalyze the underlying factual content or even put it in writing. This is often more for teacher education, where student teachers are expected to prove that they have thought about the matter, and even there, one might wonder if it really makes sense.

It is quite clear that teachers cannot teach anything that they themselves do not understand. What is meant is that they themselves must have a *virtuoso command of the things they expect of students*, that is, that they would be able to perform flawlessly on a task or test they present to their students, and that they would also be able to present several variants and solutions in each case.

PEDAGOGICAL CONTENT KNOWLEDGE (PCK): WHAT IS IT?

What we find on a subject on Wikipedia or in academic textbooks is rarely what students should and can learn. Professionals may be dealing with concepts in linguistics or proofs in higher mathematics or technologically sophisticated chemical analysis methods. Even student teachers sometimes feel that academic subject knowledge has little to do with the curriculum of the same subject.

Against better judgment, teachers and student teachers are repeatedly expected to reduce academic subject knowledge to the level of students to make it understandable. In most cases, however, this is neither possible nor useful because school knowledge that can be taught and learned is structured quite differently. The logical structure of academic knowledge is more of an obstacle to learning. This is particularly evident in content where students have everyday prior experience, especially in the natural sciences or in their native language. The knowledge that can be learned by students is materialized and elaborated in textbooks, curricula, and learning materials, but certainly not in academic literature. It is based on the profession's collective experience of how to make things teachable and learnable.

This problem was repeatedly addressed by Lee Shulman in the 1980s, who at the same time made a proposal that was to prove very productive and momentous: he postulated that between content knowledge and pedagogical knowledge there is a third domain of knowledge with its own logic. He named it "pedagogical content knowledge," or PCK for short (Shulman, 1986).

"Through PCK Shulman sought to acknowledge and represent a specialized form of professional knowledge, possessed by teachers, that sets teachers aside from other professionals. This knowledge typically grows with classroom experience and underpins how effective teachers are able to teach their subject matter in ways that support student understanding. The idea of a specialized form of professional knowledge crucial to expertise in teaching resonated well with academics, so PCK was quickly explored, adopted and adapted in a diversity of ways by researchers in the field across different domains, particularly in science and mathematics" (Hume et al., 2019, p. ix).

Especially when the students are supposed to create or discover something themselves, it would be completely wrong to think that the students can now be left to their own ideas. The great openness of discovery learning also harbors the danger of getting lost, having no idea how to proceed, and becoming discouraged. This is where the teacher's expertise is important. Without an in-depth knowledge of the pitfalls and opportunities of a task, the teacher cannot help the learner. So, the teacher needs a *thorough understanding of all facets of that specific task*, whereas in teaching, as mentioned, the general theoretical and academic knowledge of the subject does not play such a big role.

FURTHER INFORMATION AND RESOURCES

WHAT IS MEANT BY "UNDERSTANDING THE CONTENT"?

Teachers must have in-depth mastery of facts and context at the student level. They have penetrated the learning content from a wide variety of perspectives and are also familiar with different solutions, variants, and explanations. The following example comes from the highly regarded and consequential COACTIV study, which examined the relationship between teachers' competencies and students' progress in lower secondary mathematics. One of the results is highly sobering, if not shocking: for a moderately difficult task at the lower secondary level, teachers were able to give an average of just 1.15 different ways of solving it—and about one in seven teachers failed to come up with a solution at all.

Below is an excerpt from the aforementioned COACTIV study:

> Teachers should not only be able to solve tasks they use in lessons themselves, but also know different possible solutions, among other things, in order to better understand students when problems arise and to be able to provide them with adequate individual support. This was also one of the three facets of the COACTIV teaching test: generating as many possible solutions to given tasks as possible. In the following, we show one such sample task from the test. A general instruction was given in the prelude, and the neighboring numbers task was then the last of four given (see task in the box).

---

*Task for testing teacher's pedagogical
content knowledge in mathematics*

"Lucas claims that the square of a natural number is always 1
greater than the product of its two neighbors. Is Lucas's claim true?"

Please name as many different solutions as possible. Note: It
is not about guessing which solutions students would choose,
but about all possible solutions that you yourself see for this task.

Two obvious solutions for neighboring numbers are, first, an
algebraic reasoning with variables and, second, a geometric approach. The list below shows how many possible solutions to the
neighboring numbers task were written down by teachers in the
COACTIV test:

wrong solution or no solutions	16%
one correct solution	55%
two correct solutions	27%
three correct solutions	3%

The average number of correct solutions generated by teachers
was 1.15. About one in seven teachers could not indicate a correct solution at all.

Results such as this exemplify the fact that teachers' professional content knowledge appears to vary widely; other such
tasks have revealed similar or even greater differences. (Blum et
al., 2011, pp. 329–31)

Relaxed Approach to the Setting of Objectives

For the most part, experienced teachers ignore excessive demands for
objective setting, whereas they take standards—however they feel about
them—as a given and stick to them without much fuss. They make the
most of them by using them as a guideline (which is what they were created for).

One may regret the lack of enthusiasm in setting elaborate objectives,
but apparently many teachers consider it as dispensable. At the same
time, no one disputes that goals are necessary—teachers and learners
need to know where the lesson is going. The key is that many teachers
express their goals implicitly in the form of tasks, which will be discussed in
depth in later chapters.

From Linear to Flexible Planning

Metaphorically speaking, one could describe linear planning as a walk on a ridge that must be followed precisely if one does not want to fall off to the left or right. The path is precisely mapped out, both for teachers and students. Flexible planning, on the other hand, can be compared to a path formed by a network of many stepping stones leading across a pond: the stepping stones provide safety, but the path is not fixed and is only hinted at. The goal is clearly visible, but both teachers and students can vary the path, go back and forth, add additional loops.

Apparently, professional teachers largely refrain from planning lessons in a linear way; they do not try to get from A to B step by step according to the plan by staying on the predefined path. Rather, expert teachers have—in addition to prepared elements and materials—a *stock of solid, rehearsed, and promising practices* that they can fall back on whenever the situation calls for it. Again, figuratively speaking, they have many well-known islands that give them confidence; the path is not necessarily pre-planned and remains open, because they can rely on a network of points anchored on solid ground.

Dealing with Openness Thanks to Flexible Practices

In the reality of everyday school life, pedagogical situations are usually contingent, which means you can never really control what will happen next and how people will react in each case. Experienced teachers have understood that the unexpected is neither a malfunction of the lesson plan nor something alarming, but the normal case, which is usually even desired. For them, the unplannable and unexpected is something they can deal with naturally, because they know they are interacting with young people who show their spontaneous reactions, which the teacher can in turn respond to when necessary (you can call it "responsive teaching").

In such unexpected situations, knee-jerk reactions can of course be wrong, but there is no time either for in-depth analytical considerations. Therefore, the expert teacher needs a stock of flexibly deployable practices that are fueled by knowledge, routines, and, above all, sharpened intuition. For expert teachers, this *principle of flexible planning* has become the most natural thing in the world. They "play" with the prepared elements of planning and link them by means of the internalized practices. Therefore, they do not need strictly linear sequencing.

The box at the end of this chapter provides an outline of what is now understood by "core practices." Later in this book, when it comes to planning a particular lesson, we will return to the concept of core practices.

Relying on Knowledge about Students and Class

Experienced professional teachers know their students, their strengths and weaknesses, their idiosyncrasies, sometimes their character peculiarities, for which they have an understanding. They actively engage in figuring out students and, as a result, get an intuitive sense of how and how quickly to proceed.

Can student teachers also achieve this expertise in an internship or practicum? Sure, they can take big steps in this direction, if they don't just focus on themselves but instead actively engage in understanding students and invest time to do so. This practice takes practice, and it needs to start early. Knowledge about the students—in general and also about the very particular current state and difficulties—is absolutely crucial.

Those experienced teachers who are also successful expert teachers are a very important resource of knowledge and know-how that must be exploited. There is nothing wrong with learning from the experts in this field, nor is there anything wrong with teacher education being inspired by their successful practices. Particularly the model of flexible planning is successful among expert teachers. The core of the planning process is formed by the "building blocks" that competent teachers have at their disposal, whereas the prepared sequencing of activities over time is only sketchy and can be changed at any time if the situation requires it.

FURTHER INFORMATION AND RESOURCES

THIS IS WHAT WE MEAN BY "CORE PRACTICES" OF TEACHERS

The concept of core practices has received great attention recently because it has raised the prospect that teachers can use these practices to act professionally and promote learning in varying situations in daily work (Grossman, 2018; Grossman et al., 2009).

What can teachers possibly envision when we speak of the need to master a practice? We choose a very simplistic definition here: *core practices are recurring teacher activities that are important to support student progress in the best possible way.*

Core practices like "leading a classroom discussion" are essential for teaching and learning in most subjects. Most of these core practices can be well characterized, and there is much experience, research, and knowledge about them. But ultimately, they are shaped by the teacher and therefore always have an individual coloration. If teachers are interested in improving the practices, they will use them often, rehearse them, understand them better, and use them flexibly. Such practices provide teachers with a solid foundation for their professional work.

Teachers do build their practices themselves

What distinguishes practices from recipe-like recommendations? Recipes are adopted—but often lack underlying knowledge and training, and a recipe rarely tells us when it is best used and with whom. In fact, we know that the great plethora of well-intentioned advice constantly offered to teachers can be rather confusing and even discouraging.

Practices, on the other hand, must be developed from the ground up by teachers and continually improved through experience, contextual knowledge, feedback from others, reflection, and—why not—occasional practical advice. Over time, practices become second nature and so internalized that they can be used intuitively. Therefore, it is almost impossible to learn practices by copying or reading. Practices accumulate continuously the deeper you go into them. And most importantly, teachers need to fully engage with them. Ultimately, they are *their* practices for *their* teaching. Learning practices is a personal commitment of all teachers who want to improve.

There is no fast track to build practices; this is real work. This is precisely why work on core practices should be introduced in teacher education and not imposed on teachers early in their careers when they are overwhelmed with numerous other things to do. Teacher education sometimes offers opportunities to engage in practices in on-campus courses, but a particularly great potential for learning is in internships, placements in schools, and the formats that go with them. That is where practices can be focused, improved, flexibly designed, and properly trained. What helps is the support of experts in teacher education, the exchange of ideas with other prospective and experienced teachers, and the discussions with students.

Practices need knowledge and "theory"

Teachers have been confronted with a great deal of knowledge in teacher education. Most of it is relevant to the teaching profession at some point—but do teachers have the relevant knowledge at hand at the right moment? Unfortunately, all too rarely. Therefore, the essential knowledge acquired on campus and online should be merged with what teachers actually *do*.

Effective practices are based not only on experience and common sense, but also on the knowledge acquired on campus and elsewhere. It is indispensable to draw on the diverse content knowledge, pedagogical content knowledge, and educational sciences. However, it is necessary to examine which of these is useful in a specific case.

The aim is to establish *practices for the best possible professional teaching*. Teachers should ask themselves habitually whether their practices are achieving the best possible effects and whether they are up to date with relevant knowledge. The disciplines of learning and teaching and educational science are constantly researching and reviewing how schools, classrooms, and society are evolving; what concepts are promising in particular contexts; what (side) effects they have, and so forth.

Professional practices are flexible

Those who have acquired professional practices can adequately assess a situation and "see" what is going on in the first place, and then make quick and appropriate decisions depending on the situation. Take, for example, "identifying and understanding students' learning difficulties." Those who are familiar with this practice will be attentive to the students and will perceive the specifics of the present situation. They intuitively notice what is to be paid attention to, they have the appropriate knowledge and know different ways of reacting, because they have studied and trained promising strategies.

Teachers who are familiar with the practice in question know immediately what to do and what not to do. They have developed intuitions that they can rely on. In this way, they can quickly make the best possible decisions for the benefit of the students. In short: professional practices enable flexible and goal-oriented instruction, even in varying situations.

Professional practices take the pressure off the teachers

Time and again, early career teachers report that the daily challenges of school overwhelm them because they have to think about so many things they hardly had to worry about in teacher education. The professional reality is unrelenting: the teacher is constantly faced with new challenges. The pressure of time and the pressure to (re)act immediately at school triggers constant stress, which can push especially those starting out on their careers to their limits.

This is where practices help. In contrast to mere routines and rigid recommendations, they provide teachers with options to act appropriately and professionally even in stressful situations. And that is why—it is worth reiterating—it is so important that professional practices are rehearsed.

Only good practices help to achieve educational success

Last but not least: Not all practices have quality. There are also suboptimal or even harmful practices. Some practices are patterns that were not consciously designed but have formed with increasing routine. Possibly, they are not serving the goals at all. They may support the teacher in coping with everyday life, but they can also be unprofessional and counterproductive. The crucial question is: Do the practices help the teachers to fulfill their tasks as well and professionally as possible? And above all: *Do they contribute to the students' progress?* Those who develop a practice with these questions have taken an important step on the way to becoming professional teachers.

3

⚭

Rethinking Conventions of Lesson Planning

Guidelines for planning tend to be confusing as a whole. We've already seen that there seems to be no consensus on good or right planning that everyone then adheres to. Paradoxically, much of what is thought to be important is little implemented in everyday practice, and conversely, some everyday practices seem insufficiently valued by teacher education.

The goal of this book is ambitious: it seeks to outline a practice of planning that will satisfy the needs of practitioners; it also seeks to meet the demands of teacher education in introducing students to thorough planning; and, above all, this practice of planning should be entirely focused on student progress. This chapter provides an opportunity to reflect on planning habits that are so deeply embedded in the profession, some of which are to be fundamentally challenged.

SOME THINGS TO THINK ABOUT WHEN IT COMES TO LESSON PLANNING

Planning Traditions with Sometimes Unnecessary Stresses

Teachers *have to make decisions* all the time, as Madeline Hunter (1976) has repeatedly pointed out. One may disagree with some of Hunter's positions, but she is correct on this point. In planning, teachers anticipate situations and make certain decisions already beforehand; planning is, in a sense, a stockpile of decisions that teachers no longer have to make in the lesson. When reviewing the professional literature on the subject of "planning," its importance is emphasized again and again. In teacher education worldwide, it is a foregone conclusion that lesson planning is a core competence of every teacher. There is a plethora of literature that carefully explains all the issues surrounding planning in a detailed and science-based manner (e.g., Hunter, 1994; McConnell et al., 2020; Ornstein & Lasley, 2000; Stronge & Xu, 2016). Consequently, there are numerous instructions on how to ideally plan lessons.

Probably most teachers can confirm that planning lessons triggers ambivalent reactions. Less experienced teachers have to consider all too many things with which they are not yet familiar. In teacher education, there are also expectations of cooperating teachers and teacher educators to be met; numerous important cues and rules are to be followed. All of this makes planning more complex: one time you have too many ideas, the next you have none at all. Sometimes it is expected to plan ahead precisely and to formulate objectives in detail; in other contexts, flexibility and improvisation are required. In short, planning lessons is generally accepted as a necessity, but it is associated with many contradictions and is often experienced as a burden.

For student teachers, planning means not only preparing a specific unit or lesson, but also proving that you are capable of applying theoretical knowledge in a practical way: "Lesson planning is one aspect of teacher education in which pre-service teachers have the ability to apply the instructional strategies, content-based pedagogy and educational theory they have learned in their coursework to classroom practice" (Vermette et al., 2010, p. 70).

If student teachers do not present elaborate planning, they might give the impression that they have not dealt enough with subsequent teaching. Planning is often interpreted in teacher education as evidence of one's commitment, and student teachers who do not write down and justify their ideas may be suspected of sloppiness. But perhaps student teachers do behave rationally, as Oelkers (2009) puts it: "The focus of teachers' work is on instruction-related activities. Anything that increases effort without improving output will not find use in this practice" (p. 9). And Werner et al. (2017) soberly note that even "poorly planned lessons can succeed" (p. 105).

Let us take objective setting as an example. Studies and reports in recent decades complain that student teachers are insufficiently concerned with objectives, whereas virtually all planning schemes put objective setting first (e.g., Jones et al., 2011; Orlich et al., 2004; Ornstein & Lasley, 2000; Sánchez & Valcárcel, 1999; Zahorik, 1975). In fact, objective setting is not a priority for student teachers because they are primarily concerned with what they should *do* and what students should *do*. Starting with objectives misses the real needs and wants of student teachers entirely.

An up-to-date planning approach must have a convincing answer to this discrepancy.

In this way, student teachers can become alienated from the planning requirements of teacher education because they experience them as not really serving their daily work. Wernke and Zierer (2017) state: "If . . . planning in the context of teacher education is perceived as something that is of no use, in which one finds no sense, which only bullies one, then it is not surprising if later it is no longer resorted to in an intensive way" (p. 14).

Tendency to Overestimate Oneself

But there's another problem that is rooted in the teachers themselves.

It may be that less experienced teachers and student teachers avoid thorough planning and limit it to a few notes because they simply overestimate themselves with regard to their own teaching skills. Addressing this problem can make student teachers uncomfortable at times, but it is important to call a spade a spade: it's about *amateurish improvisation*. Everyone thinks they know how "to do it" because what goes on in classes is deeply culturally embedded knowledge. Even young children have an idea of what school is like, and so the students usually play along in the game called "class."

Unfortunately, inexperienced teachers in particular are tempted to overestimate their competencies and skills. When lessons are more or less orderly, they get the impression that they have mastered the craft of planning and teaching. Planning is then minimalistic, even if background knowledge is poor and experience is insufficient to react flexibly according to the situation. It may be that student teachers, when improvising, unconsciously fall back on patterns of teaching that they themselves have experienced as students. Perhaps they get through the lessons this way, but this has little to do with professional teaching that wants to ensure progress for the students.

Planning to Reduce Complexity and Gain Control?

From the student teacher's perspective, careful planning provides some reassurance. If, due to lack of experience, it is uncertain how the lesson will go, one is glad to be able to stick to a detailed lesson plan. The result, of course, is a fairly teacher-centered lesson, but in return, the complexity of the lesson is greatly reduced, and control over what happens is rather increased. This allows teachers to better channel what is happening to avoid undesirable courses of events. A lesson planned in detail can reduce the risk of getting overwhelmed.

There is nothing wrong with a helpful reduction of complexity. Concerns should only be raised in the case that planning is overdetailed and controls the lesson too rigidly. This tendency is exacerbated by the presence of visitors (mentors, cooperating teachers, etc.), and especially when teacher performance is evaluated. That's when you want to reduce the risks of unplanned mishaps as much as possible. To avoid failures in an exam-like situation, one tends to "overplan."

But is the effort for more control and less contingency justified? There are two things to consider: (1) the effort is huge to anticipate multiple possible scenarios and come up with a course of action for each, and (2) students' reactions, moods, and thoughts are rarely truly predictable, and therefore rigid implementation of planning risks leaving no room for students and may silence their voices.

Linear Planning as an Obstacle on the Way to Student-Centered Teaching

The abovementioned tendency to control refers to the "surface structure" of teaching (Oser & Baeriswyl, 2001), that is, to all visible processes in a classroom. Of course, it is not enough to control everything visible (although novices in particular are inclined to this misconception). But linear planning patterns that dictate step by step the course of the lesson tend to do just that. When students behave unpredictably, it is then often seen as something negative, a disruption.

In linearly planned instruction, the well-oiled mechanics of the lesson take priority over educational effects on students. This is where the contradictions of rigid planning come to the fore: it has long become commonplace to think of teaching from the students' perspective, from their learning. Those who strive for student-oriented teaching that gives room to the individual thinking, feeling, and acting of all young people must recognize that it *cannot be planned completely* in its details and flow.

The notion of linear lesson planning is inherently rooted in the student teachers' own school experiences of teaching as a flowing linear process. But twentieth-century teacher education practices also have their share. Formalistic exaggerations of planning no longer seem appropriate, and the pressure to plan lessons in detail is probably much less today. Detailed planning is far from being good planning, and good planning does not have to be highly elaborate but must comprehensibly present the key considerations that are to lead to sustainable learning. Not everything needs to be laid out in advance, which is better decided as the lesson progresses. The linear aspect of planning can ultimately be limited to a few milestones and may have the *character of an outline* that allows for the flexible use of planning elements.

Oversimplified Planning Templates

Understandably, teachers and student teachers are looking for expedient and work-efficient aids. It is common practice (and mostly supported by teacher education) for student teachers to use planning templates along which they can work through point by point. If you search for such planning templates, you will find thousands of them and in a wide variety of printed or digital versions (see figure 3.1).

Using a template is certainly a quite pragmatic working aid. It is understandable and useful that teachers somehow rationalize their lesson planning. But the question is what ideas and principles underlie such a template, and what effects they have. Will teaching automatically improve if you use the "right" template?

Remarkably, most lesson planning templates follow a similar basic pattern. Norm Friesen (2010), after reviewing planning practices in the Anglo-Saxon world, states: "The development of lesson plans through the use of planning templates is a central part of teacher preparation programs in the United Kingdom, Canada and the United States. More-

Name: Placement:	Lesson evaluation: Date:
Objectives	
Timing	
Grouping	
Differentiation	
Whole class	
Assessment of outcomes	
Successes	Action plan
Difficulties:	

LESSON PLAN Ref:		Course Ref:
Subject / Course:		
Topic:		
Lesson Title:		
Level:		Duration:
Lesson Objectives:		
Summary of Tasks / Actions:		
Materials / Equipment:		
References:		
Take Home Tasks:		

Figure 3.1. Two common examples of lesson plan templates. On the left, a typical example according to John (2006, p. 485); on the right, a downloadable example from https://www.class-templates.com/.

over, the basic designs of these templates vary surprisingly little from country to country" (p. 417). Not only practical guides, but also academic publications repeatedly address the question of how such formalized planning procedures could be improved (e.g., Causton-Theoharis et al., 2008; Ornstein, 1997; Vermette et al., 2010).

John (2006) and Friesen (2010) note that there is a strong emphasis on effective teaching and, in the context of planning, there are many direct or indirect references to the same authors who incorporate the effective teaching approach into their concepts and planning recommendations. Notable among these are Tyler (1949), Bloom et al. (1956), Gagné (1974), and Hunter (1994). The unifying feature of these approaches is the focus on effective teaching and the reference to psychological knowledge from behaviorist and cognitivist perspectives. With the constructivist turn toward the end of the last century, the approach of coherent instruction and ensuring optimal learning conditions was not fundamentally questioned, but "blind spots" were pointed out, in particular the need to take into account the individual and social construction of knowledge in student learning—something beyond the direct control of teachers (e.g., Berg & Clough, 1991; Uhrmacher et al., 2013).

Many planning templates—and this is now the point—reflect an overly mechanistic understanding of teaching and learning. They are sometimes understood as a promise or even a guarantee that success will come to those who follow the prescribed steps exactly—although this is certainly not what most authors intended. When we look at planning in the following chapters, we will have to beware of this trap.

Activities and Suggestions

PLANNING: YOUR EXPERIENCES AND CURRENT IDEAS

Keywords to Your Preconcept of Planning

Generally, in teacher education, concepts of lesson planning are imposed on student teachers, determining the guidelines by which student teachers invest their time in planning. Undoubtedly, this triggers reactions that reverberate well into the profession. Hence the following proposal for taking stock.

Write down spontaneously in as many keywords as possible what comes to your mind on the topic of lesson planning:

Now sift through the keywords according to the aspects below and try to get an overall picture. For this purpose, you can mark the keywords with corresponding colors, for example, or make notes in a column on the right.

Overall picture:

Are the majority of the keywords rather neutral, or do they have a positive or negative undertone?

Emotions:

To what extent do the keywords primarily relate to your (emotional) reactions to the topic of planning?

Predetermined elements:

Did you also note specific elements of planning (e.g., analysis of content, detailed objectives, reference to given standards, assignment)?

Theoretical concepts:

Did any rather theoretical planning concepts come to mind that were recommended to be applied at some point?

Process of planning:

Have you written down aspects that concern your own planning routines, for example, effort, level of detail?

Practical preparation:

To what extent are practical preparations represented, for example, acquiring and providing materials, planning tasks and activities, writing texts, preparing visualizations?

Other:

Are there any aspects noted that do not fall into any of the above categories?

Current Status: What Aspects about Planning
Do You Pay Particular Attention To?

Go through the keywords and the markers again, and identify a maximum of three noteworthy aspects—namely, what is a problem or a burden, or on the contrary, what gives you pleasure and what you feel competent in?

4

⚛️

The Key Principle of
Planning Units Backward

As we know, a large number of planning recommendations and templates are available. Do we really need another approach called backward planning? No, it's just a simple principle of planning that is fundamental to professional, focused, lean, efficient, and student-centered planning. Backward planning changes direction from forward planning, as the name implies, and begins with what is expected to be the outcome of the learning processes. The backward planning approach is by no means new, but since given standards for teaching and learning play an increasingly important role, it has become more familiar to teachers.

Backward planning belongs to the category of those things that are amazingly simple and obvious. The basic idea succeeds in implementing the key expectations of professional teaching, namely, focus on goals, on students, their competencies, and on standards and curricula, and does so in a labor-efficient manner.

WHAT IS BACKWARD PLANNING
(AS OPPOSED TO FORWARD PLANNING)?

The basic idea of backward planning has already been briefly outlined in the first chapter (see figure 1.1). We will now take a closer look at it here. Everyone is familiar with traditional forward planning: teachers develop a learning opportunity, and then they review the learning outcomes. Backward planning means reversing the order and planning the end first.

The basic idea is very simple: *before planning lessons and learning processes, the teacher determines the desired outcomes and how to check them.*

Imagine a teacher who says, "The first thing I do when I tackle a new topic is write the final test or exam or whatever you want to call it. I spend quite a bit of time and energy writing fair tasks. The tasks should be solvable, not trivial, and by solving them, students can demonstrate what they understand about the subject. Then, when the students master it at the end of the unit, we are all satisfied; we have met or perhaps exceeded the goals. When I have put these tasks together, I know where the journey is going, and I communicate it to the students. When we—the students and I—have the tasks of the final test in mind, we can work more purposefully and efficiently."

This teacher may never have heard of backward planning, but they implement the basic idea perfectly. This approach is logical and absolutely rational, and it may come as a surprise that not all teachers do it this way.

Here now, in summary, this planning principle, which consists of three steps:

1. *Defining desired outcomes on a topic* (goals, competencies to be acquired in a given time frame)
2. *Elaborating on the assessment and tasks for the learning and assessment* (e.g., tests, activities, series of tasks, specific performance target, precise quality criteria, etc.) based on in-depth knowledge of the focused topic
3. *Planning lessons, learning opportunities, and support* (so that in the end the assessment will be successful)

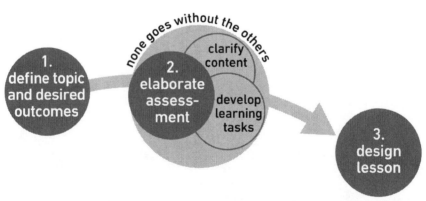

Figure 4.1.   The principle of backward planning. *Created by the author*

The Origins of the Idea of Planning Backward

Whenever one has a product to complete at a certain point in time or a process to finish, it is advisable to calculate back from the end point to plan the process in a meaningful way. This basic idea of backward planning has been in use in many fields for a long time (film studies: e.g., Rose, 1962; logistics: e.g., Bowers, 1971; production planning: e.g., Andersson et al., 1980; education system and curricula: e.g., McDonald, 1992). For instruction, such approaches can be found as early as Tyler (1949). He emphatically stressed the importance of accurate evaluation, that is, a review that best reflects the objectives. Precise and at all times transparent formulations of intent were also demanded by Mager (1962).

However, it was not until Wiggins and McTighe (1998, 2006, 2011) that the approach of backward planning or backward design was consistently taken to its full potential as a method of planning for instruction. It is to the great credit of these two authors that they have elaborated and convincingly presented the basic idea of backward planning in a series of books that revolve around the concept of "understanding by design."

This now means that instruction and learning activities are specified only after it is crystal clear what is to be achieved in the end and with which tasks it is assessed—not in general statements of goals, but in precisely described actions. Once this is done, there is little doubt about what is to be learned, what is relevant, what is to be achieved at what level, and so forth. Everyone knows what is important—the teacher and the learners.

Table 4.1 compares the two planning principles, forward planning" and backward planning. If you are not yet familiar with backward planning, you are advised to read the right-hand column of table 4.1 step by step and to follow it mentally.

Delivering Lessons Forward Misses Either the Students or the Objectives

It is a long-standing call to first establish the goals or define desired competencies. In this era when goals and standards are being formulated more rigorously than ever, backward planning should actually become increasingly mainstream.

If this approach is really put into practice, it is replacing the strong tradition of "teaching first" and then determining the nature and content of assessment. In the teaching first tradition, many teachers have focused first on the successful flow of instruction ("smooth running," McDonald, 1992), and then considered the review of learning. From the teachers' point of view, this is understandable, because teaching triggers greater pressure to act than testing. And yet the sequence is wrong and causes difficulties for both teacher and learner:

In the logic of forward planning, the teacher faces a dilemma. The teacher may say that to be fair, only what has been covered may be tested. The teacher will consider what has been dealt with and what has been addressed rather marginally or not at all, even though it was intended to be. If the teacher is testing only what has been covered in real terms, they move away from what was actually intended, and the objectives are missed.

On the other hand, if the teacher accurately tests what corresponds to the original objectives, they may ignore what the students have actually learned. The teacher may stick to the predefined objectives and will be able to say to what extent they have been achieved, but this may be very unfair because perhaps the learning opportunities were not sufficient for the students to achieve the objectives in the first place.

In other words, if the teacher practices forward planning, that is, just teaching and worrying about assessment later, there will almost certainly be a mismatch between the goals and what is actually learned, and the result will be that either the goals will be missed, or the students will be wronged (or both).

Success Criteria Are Clarified First: Students Know What Matters

If the assessment is clear from the outset, that is, if the teacher has something like a final test in hand from the start, they are not teaching blindly, but can *put all energy in the service of student success*. "Student success" in the broader sense means progress in the cognitive, social, affective, and motor domains, that, not just in the cognitive performance of selected subjects, as is often perceived in a truncated way.

Verifiable success criteria are much more concrete than mere statements of goals. It is not enough to state goals and then teach as usual without the goals being present in the classroom. In the dynamic of backward planning, the teacher is much more scrupulous and thinks carefully about what students should achieve and how *everyone can check progress at any time*, both the teacher and the students themselves.

"Assessing" means, above all, finding out where we stand

If the teacher has final assessment tasks at hand and is guided by them, it does not mean that a final test must be imposed at all costs. After all, assessment tasks primarily have a guiding function for teaching and learning. Assessing does not always mean "testing," as we know, but finding out where we stand. It may or may not be summative and evaluative; it does not have to be graded. Test items and tasks can be used in many ways:

- Formative
- As self-assessments
- As assessments in a conversation between teacher and student
- As products that are appreciated by the teacher

Thus, assessment simply provides an answer to the question "Where am I in relation to the goals?"

The point is, *everything must be out in the open from the beginning*, all self-assessment options, all expectations, testing procedures, testing requirements, performance standards, and criteria. The teacher does not hide any test items from the students. Everyone knows what is important for them to succeed. Backward planning is thus inextricably linked to the intention to consistently make student progress the starting and ending point of all teaching.

All just "teaching to the test"? A misunderstanding

One serious objection to backward planning is that teachers now would teach only what will be tested at the end, and students, too, focus only on topics that will be tested. Instruction, it is argued, is narrowly focused with the tests in mind. As a result, all learning and discovery that is not strictly tested would be devalued and would hardly be given any space or appreciation.

There are good reasons to counter this objection:

1. The "teaching to the test" argument refers to externally imposed standards and curricula, which are the reality of the current school system. Performance on this predetermined content has immediate consequences for children, teachers, and schools. Whether one likes it or not, teachers, students, and parents have to submit to this reality. In the end, it is entirely rational to prepare for the tests in the best possible way.
2. Even though standards and tests are a reality in schools, no teacher will use the entire instructional time as training for the tests. Teachers have a lot of leeway to address other issues as well and to enrich the curriculum with relevant and motivating topics.
3. A common prejudice is that test items are restrictive, and students are usually only addressed at a lower cognitive level of Bloom's

taxonomy, for example, reproducing facts. We will discuss taxonomies of objectives later. Here is just this for now:

- The teacher can open up the spectrum, especially with testing;
  they can also set challenging and open tasks. Teachers can address social, physical, and emotional dimensions in addition to
  cognitive ones. It would be fundamentally wrong to think that
  assessment should consist of test items that are not cognitively demanding and leave out important noncognitive areas of personal
  development.
- Today, challenging standards are set that address students not
  only at the level of basic skills and factual knowledge. Example:
  In the Common Core State Standards for math, there is a keyword
  "understanding." To meet these types of standards, teachers must
  not only find intelligent tasks, but also design responsive and dis-
  cursive instruction.
- Most importantly, teachers have precisely with the backward
  planning a tool to extend the learning processes to all levels that
  seem important to them—by offering appropriate tasks on these
  challenging levels for assessment.
4. Incidental learning—that is, unintended and consequently untested
   learning—always takes place. It is not hindered by teaching that
   seeks to achieve measurable results.

CONVINCING ADVANTAGES OF BACKWARD PLANNING

The backward planning approach may take some getting used to. Many
teachers are more familiar with the "delivering lessons mode" and are
not in the habit of looking at the assessment in detail right at the start of
planning. But the consistent shift pays off in several ways:

1. **At the same time a precise definition of objectives**—That a teacher
   must decide on a topic is self-evident. Backward planning addition-
   ally requires that the intentions are also clarified briefly, understandably, and credibly. Further detailed definitions of goals, on the other
   hand, are unnecessary if they are included in the assessment, that is,
   if they are materialized in tasks, assignments, and so forth with the
   corresponding criteria for success.
2. **At the same time an in-depth analysis of content**—As discussed
   earlier, analysis of content means that the teacher has a flexible command of the subject matter as it is to be acquired by the students. By
   engaging in in-depth assessment, the teacher inevitably closes their
   own gaps in understanding and knowledge.

Table 4.1. The assessment as a pivot for planning and teaching: comparison of the planning process of forward and backward planning.

Starting point: A teacher plans a larger unit in a given time frame, for example, four weeks in math, PE, language, or history.

	Forward Planning	Backward Planning
Step 1	**Topic and contents** The teacher decides on a topic by exploring what they want or need to "cover."	**Topic and core intentions/goals** The teacher decides on a topic and at the same time elaborates on its central purpose, namely, the core of what learners should be engaged in and what should ultimately stick. In other words, a specific picture of the *expected results* is formed.
Step 2	**Planning lesson, supporting learning** Transferring the topic to the lesson: The teacher reflects on • how to design the lesson with this topic; • what activities could be stimulating, interesting, and useful to get the learners to engage with the topic; and • what the students could learn from this topic. Based on these decisions, the teacher plans the inputs, learning materials, and activities.	**Elaborate assessment** *Design assessment*: • The teacher reflects how it will be possible to tell at the end if these central things have been learned. • They do so in *designing an accurate assessment of what is to be learned*, that is, designing specific tasks, situations, and assignments for assessment, and doing so in ample quantity. • The teacher simultaneously deepens their professional understanding of the topic, if necessary. *Critically analyze and rewrite assessment*: • The teacher examines whether the tasks and assignments really test what is important to them (e.g., comprehension rather than rote memorization; problem solving rather than rote computation; productive rather than competitive collaboration). • The teacher changes the assessment until it calls out exactly what they think is important. The teacher has now aligned assessment with essential intentions and, at the same time, has made the goals as visible as possible and has at the same time created tasks for learning activities.
Step 3	**Elaborate assessment** The teacher reflects on • how to review what the students have learned about the topic; and • what kind of tasks, activities, and so forth are appropriate for this purpose. The teacher works out the assessment by matching it to what has been covered.	**Planning the lesson, supporting learning** • The teacher consistently plans inputs, learning materials, and activities so that students can learn exactly what is the subject of the assessment. • The teacher provides learning opportunities so that students can actually get there, using the assessment tasks as well. *Transparency of intentions or goals and assessment*: • To this end, the teacher makes completely transparent what is expected of students at the end. • All students know what will be tested and how (including any tasks that could be used as assessments), meaning they learn what needs to be done to be successful.

Created by the author.

3. **Pragmatic and work efficient**—Backward planning recognizes that the pragmatic planning of truly expert teachers contains all the important elements of professional planning. Therefore, pro forma elements can be omitted if they are not really functional for teaching. If teacher take the assessment seriously and work it out at the beginning, they have already laid the groundwork for almost all of the planning:

   By elaborating a consistent assessment right at the beginning of the planning process, the teacher
   - specifies the objectives and deepens the content,
   - develops appropriate activities and tasks for learning and for assessment, and
   - already creates the basis for a stringent lesson plan and does not have to think about what should be "delivered."

4. **More relaxing for students**—What teacher hasn't heard questions from students of this sort: "Do we need to know it for the test?" This may annoy some teachers, but the question is perfectly rational. Teachers can intelligently take advantage of this test orientation by generating challenging tasks and questions to direct student interest. Ultimately, it is a boon for students to know what matters and what they need to learn to be successful.

5

∞

Planning a Unit

Before we get back to lesson planning, let's talk about *planning a unit*, that is, a series of several lessons on a topic, which can sometimes span several weeks. The planning principles of backward planning are the same as for a lesson, and yet unit planning has some unique features:

- In unit planning, you adopt the *perspective of the requirements* (standards, curriculum); later you will look at the particular lessons from the perspective of the students. So, unit planning is a *top-down process* with the question "How do I bring the predefined requirements into the classroom?"
- In unit planning, you make *curricular decisions*: What standards do I want students to meet? What content do I address?
- In unit planning, you set *your own priorities*: What can I bring in myself? Where (in the context of this topic) can the students benefit from me?
- And most importantly: in unit planning, you *design tasks* that the students should master at the end.

So, you could say: When planning a unit, we think "from above," from the specifications. What do the mandatory standards require? What topics must be addressed? What skills, what knowledge, what insights must be acquired? What is important from the teacher's point of view? Don't worry: the students' perspective (their needs, their questions, their interests, their capacities) are then central to the planning of the specific lessons. More on that later.

A LEAN PLANNING PRACTICE

Planning tools should support the teacher, but should neither be trivializing planning nor be perceived as a burden or harassment. The heuristics discussed here show how unit planning can be made more essential and result in a rational, expedient, and lean planning practice. Three claims are made for such unit planning practice: unit planning *clarifies a few basic things*; it does the *major preparatory work*; and it is *purposeful and expedient*.

The backward planning process outlined earlier meets these expectations of stringent and lean planning: after basic decisions about the *content and the intentions* or goals (what outcome is to be achieved?), the *assessment* is worked out in detail—and thus everything that follows is established in principle. Figure 5.1 shows the workflow of the planning process for a thematic unit. The simple model of backward planning already presented in figure 4.1 can be seen here; it is just enriched by some elements: in (1) for the definition of the topic and the desired outcome, the sources are indicated; in (2) it is emphasized again that the assessment is inseparable from the clarification of the content and the elaboration of tasks; and (3) is a preview of the design of the lesson, which also includes the student perspective.

As stated, a unit spans several lessons. Once the basic work of unit planning is done, the division into subunits emerges naturally by setting a manageable and achievable learning focus for each lesson, and the lesson design can already be sketched in broad strokes.

MORE ESSENTIAL—WITHOUT LOSS OF SUBSTANCE

The proposed scheme for planning units is lean and follows—after viewing the standards and the curriculum—two steps:

1. The *basic decisions* of the teacher on intentions and topic and desired results
2. *Working out the assessment* in terms of tasks and activities that also serve as learning opportunities

Those familiar with other planning templates will miss a few things. One might assume that the main focus on topics and activities trivializes planning and ignores essential questions. Planning, someone might argue, is reduced to a quasi-technological process that boils down to skills and knowledge and their assessment. One might also object that it is negligent to jettison the familiar elements of planning, such as carefully elaborating goals or eliciting students' prior knowledge.

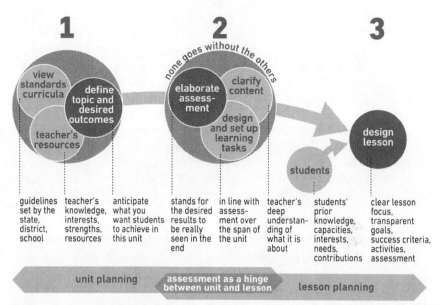

Figure 5.1. Workflow of planning a thematic unit over several lessons. *Created by the author*

Yet these aspects are not at all neglected, even though they are not explicitly listed. These aspects are simply addressed in the presented strategy in an unconventional way. The basic idea here is that the planning teacher cannot help but necessarily include the seemingly missing aspects in the regular course of pragmatic planning. Whoever conscientiously plans in this way must deal with the subject matter, the objectives, prior knowledge, conditions, and so forth.

Not Necessary: Extensively Analyze the Underlying Content

The analysis and understanding of content take place implicitly repeatedly. First, when teachers look at the subject and decide what is to be learned; further, teachers will delve deeper into the material to be learned when they are planning activities, designing or selecting tasks, and making sure that they have understood them in depth and will be able to effectively help students work with them.

Certainly, teachers and especially student teachers can be careless on this point, but let us assume that teachers have the decency and ethical attitude to want to understand the subject matter themselves, which they offer to the students as an object of learning. And teacher educators are well advised to rigorously insist that student teachers absolutely understand the content at the students' level and can themselves solve the tasks they give students.

Thorough analyses of the content are already available for almost all topics. This is the field of the experts for teaching and learning and the authors of teaching materials. These experts have invested a great deal of their own expertise and time to penetrate a subject matter and present it in such a way that it becomes learnable. This knowledge is available and should be used. It is usually unnecessary and unproductive for teachers to start from scratch; this only makes sense for a very few current topics for which no prepared material is yet available. This knowledge prepared for teaching and learning is called pedagogical content knowledge (PCK), which was discussed earlier in this book.

Not Necessary: Define Detailed Objectives

The detailed objectives are specified implicitly, but in a way that is easy to understand, because in every task, in every assignment, in every activity there is an intention, that is, a goal. *The tasks represent the desired outcomes.* It is then clear to the students (and to the teacher): what this task asks shows what the goal of the whole undertaking is.

However, we assume that the teacher conscientiously constructs or selects the tasks. The tasks must demand exactly what is to be learned, that is, what the goal is. If teachers were to superficially put together a few tasks without being aware of what is being learned, then both student activities and goals would become largely random. This is definitely not how it should be.

Not Necessary at This Point: Consider in Detail Students' Prior Knowledge and Conditions

To be clear, it is, of course, important that learning connect to the prior knowledge of each student and take into account the specific conditions of everyone—but not in unit planning. Here, we consider what the class as a whole has already worked on and what inherent logic the content follows. For example, a teacher will address adding fractions only after students have worked on how to reduce fractions to the same common denominator.

When the next step will be to plan the specific lesson, these aspects— prior knowledge and special situations of the students—will be especially important to ensure learning success. But more on that later (see also box).

These Questions Remain Open for the Time Being

Some questions must at this point remain unanswered, particularly regarding the choice of intentions, goals, topic, and activities. Therefore, later chapters will be devoted to these areas.

What about standards and other predetermined goals and content?

In most cases, teachers are expected to adhere to predetermined state, district, or school standards. These specifications are an important guide in planning courses and the schemes of work that teachers use to structure instruction for longer periods of time—half a year or a full year. In this chapter, we are only discussing the planning of a unit that focuses on *one* topic, assuming that the teacher has already decided on a topic.

And what about the students' prior knowledge and interests?

All teachers today know that there is a wide range of prior knowledge, abilities, and interests in every class. Any teacher interested in student progress needs to know this and base their planning on it.

These aspects hardly come into play in unit planning, but they very much do later when planning the *specific lesson*. Knowing how the students are doing at that particular moment, the teacher will plan adaptively.

With this pragmatic two-step procedure of "topic/desired outcomes" and "assessment/tasks," it can be avoided that the recommended planning elements are merely written down as a matter of formality and remain ineffective (or are skipped with a guilty conscience). It is not a matter of thinning out unit planning, but on the contrary, of integrating the central elements into a consistent process. The scheme does not call for superfluous planning prose that countless student teachers would rightly struggle with.

UNIT PLANNING: A SET OF TASKS
THAT LEAD TO THE DESIRED OUTCOMES

We are talking here about a fairly radical transformation of a planning tradition that was essentially focused on instructional delivery and instructional control into a contemporary, expedient, and pragmatic practice of planning that both focuses on learning opportunities and facilitates teacher-friendly ways of working.

Like anything people do, unit planning can be done carefully, seriously, and thoughtfully, or it can be done sloppily, minimally, and thoughtlessly.

- In the desirable case of careful planning, a thoughtful pool of tasks emerges that fit the topic and are appropriate for learning and assessing what is desired. The tasks are the materialization of both the topic and the intentions, that is, what should be the final outcome.
- In the undesirable case of careless planning, the teacher simply puts together a bunch of tasks to keep the students busy, without really knowing what they have to learn and whether the tasks will help them or not.

Therefore, good planning that is conducive to learning only results when a teacher wants the best and is conscientious and committed to getting things done. What this book can do is merely offer promising planning heuristics that are resource efficient yet professional, but whether teachers implement them well must be up to them.

The Task Stands for Goals and Content: An Example

Further above, it was justified why the detailed objectives do not need to be spelled out, since they are materialized in the tasks. This example can illustrate that the tasks do of course contain the objectives, and that this is useful for both learners and teachers. Imagine the following scenario where the teacher has decided on a topic and some desired outcomes.

Look at table 5.1 and imagine if a completely different task had been set. Suppose the teacher had the above intent, but the task was, "Name the year the Panama Canal was built, the number of locks, and the average passage time." This would only test factual knowledge. However, the teacher's actual intention, a deeper understanding of the functions of the canal, is not addressed at all. The goal and the task are not congruent. The students learn the "wrong" thing, that is, something that was not intended in the first place, or—even worse—they are tested on something that was definitely not learned. In any case, the learning effort goes nowhere, and the result is usually frustration and failure.

The Variety of Goals and the Tasks to Match Them: How to Proceed?

Goals (= expected results) are always linked to tasks, as we have now noted several times. Banal goals necessitate banal tasks, and challenging goals necessitate challenging tasks. And vice versa: demanding tasks require that the teacher sets more demanding goals. Crossed doesn't work:

Table 5.1. The tasks as the core of unit planning. Example: "International Trade Routes."

Steps of Unit Planning	Elaboration	Comments
Topic and Desired Outcome	*The topic:* International trade routes *A desired outcome:* Students know the location and features of some major international trade routes and have formed an opinion about the extent to which they are significant and why this is so.	Up to this point, this is the first step in unit planning. After reviewing the standards and curriculum, the teacher decides that international trade routes are an important topic and that students should know about them, do their own research and thinking about their importance, and be able to communicate those thoughts.
Tasks	*A learning focus for a task:* Panama Canal and potential consequences of a closure	This kind of topic is still quite unspecific and needs to get more fleshed out, because tasks are always about something very specific. In this case, the teacher chooses the Panama Canal as the learning focus (another route would also be possible, but the teacher already has in-depth knowledge about the Panama Canal).
	The task (given to the students): Research what the consequences of a (hypothetical) closure of the Panama Canal would be in the short, medium, and long term for shipping routes; the supply of goods; the global economy in general; and what policy issues might arise. Hints: • Do some research on how the Panama Canal is used, by whom, and for what purposes. • Look for similar events in the past where trade routes were disrupted. This may give you clues for this task. • Present your insights in a way that is easily understood and followed by others.	Elaborate a task where students can learn what is desired: Tasks should be set to reflect the teacher's intent. If this is the case, then students know what they face; *the goal is clear to the learners.* The task implicitly tells learners what they are expected to learn, for example, do research, find meaningful maps and compare their significance, look for helpful news, perhaps even talk or write to experts, make comparisons with similar events, find and be able to use a website about trade routes, read and interpret statistics about shipping routes, draw reasoned conclusions.
Tasks for Assessments	*Analogous tasks* with the same intent that can be used for both learning and assessment	The congruence of the learning tasks and the test tasks is absolutely important because that is precisely how students understand what is to be learned and how their progress will be checked.

challenging goals and banal tasks tend to underchallenge students, and banal goals with challenging tasks tend to overchallenge most students. Both frustrate and make no sense. Tasks should be such that all students can make real progress with them. How to match the level of challenge with the students' capabilities is something we will see subsequently in lesson planning.

But the question remains: How does one construct or find the tasks that match the expected outcomes? The example of table 5.1 shows that there is a wide range of goals and corresponding tasks, from simple factual knowledge to complex problem solving. In addition, the expected outcomes should be aligned with the specifications of the standards and so forth. Setting goals and matching tasks at the right levels of expectation is so important that it is covered in depth in separate chapters later in this book.

Planning a Unit in Teacher Education

Student teachers only occasionally find themselves in the situation of planning entire thematic units for practicum. However, planning a unit for a practicum is little different from the procedure described here. In practice, of course, students discuss the basic decisions (intentions, topic, learning focus, tasks) with the teacher in whose class the lesson is to take place. Everything else is to be agreed upon situationally. If this approach of backward planning causes irritation for cooperating teachers, the best thing to do is to address the issue openly and find a way that satisfies all sides.

In teacher education, it is not uncommon for student teachers to have to plan entire units that are not directly tied to teaching in a practicum. This allows them to delve into a topic from a subject-specific perspective, free from immediate pressure to act. These are often exemplary and detailed in-depth studies to better understand certain content-related and learning-related characteristics of the subject. Regardless of the customs in the particular subject or level, it is also advisable to proceed backward, starting with the desired outcomes and carefully planning step by step according to the above scheme. It is a good opportunity to familiarize yourself with this planning approach.

6

⧜

Planning a Lesson Backward

Lesson planning should be a real help for the teacher, not a burden. Therefore, planning should be easy; the considerations should not be overcomplex. In the classroom, prepared planning should support flexible and professional teaching and lead to student success. Thus, lesson planning here has a twofold ambition: (1) primarily, a *professional* one: planning should enable successful learning, and (2) secondly, a *pragmatic* one: planning can be prepared and carried out with a reasonable effort.

Therefore, the process of planning a lesson must be focused, lean, flexible, and student centered. Lesson planning, as presented here, is quite different from many commonly used procedures. For a moment, don't think about what you usually do or what has been recommended to you, but simply follow the reasoning behind this approach.

Another preliminary remark and advice: this procedure is aimed at teachers who are in the profession and usually work alone. In-service teachers and even prospective teachers in internship usually cannot count on the help of peers; they do the planning alone and are responsible for it. But because much about backward planning is new, it is strongly advised to plan a few units and lessons together with peers to support each other and avoid falling back into old patterns. Recommendations on how to plan in teacher education and to learn how to plan productively will be the subject of the next chapter.

THREE FOUNDATIONS FOR PLANNING A LESSON

This approach is based on a few essentials, which will be recalled and explained as we now delve into lesson planning. Three things should be at hand: unit planning, a basic formal framework for lessons, and teacher practices. All three are briefly explained here.

Foundation 1: The Unit Plan

We assume that unit planning has usually already been done—rarely does a lesson stand alone; usually it is embedded in a series of lessons on an overarching topic. In unit planning, especially if it has been done as suggested in the previous chapter, the topic is outlined and, most importantly, there is a set of tasks that guide the lessons that follow.

For the particular lesson, this means: the teacher chooses a *focus within the topic*. If we take the example of international trade routes that we explained in the previous chapter: the focus for this lesson is investigating the importance of trade routes using the Panama Canal as an example. The teacher can stick to the prepared tasks since the tasks are coherent— they address both the main content and the desired outcomes (synonymous with the goals). These tasks are, so to speak, the backbone of the lesson. They contain everything essential in a condensed form.

Foundation 2: Basic Structure of Lessons

A second foundation is a simple lesson structure that is applicable to the vast majority of lessons and is not restrictive but merely helpful. The main characteristic of the lesson here is that it takes place in a limited time frame, and this time must somehow be structured in a meaningful way.

Structuring teaching in phases is nothing new and originally results from the logic of a lesson. Herbart, a German pedagogue of the nineteenth century, who was also highly regarded in the Anglo-Saxon world (e.g., Dodd, 1898), had already advocated phases in teaching with his formal stage theory (cf. Compayré, 1908). Much fuss was made about such models of instructional design during the last century. In times when the more or less strict guidance of instruction by teachers prevailed, much was invested in variations of artful staging, not least because it was associated with the expectation that the right phasing scheme would be essential to achieving goals. Learning was supposed to be optimally supported by the given sequencing.

In the meantime, there is considerable skepticism with regard to such expectations, even if the advantages of certain teaching concepts continue to be eagerly promoted. Today, the dominant idea is rather that the progress of students does not depend so much on the external staging as on what happens inside the students, and to what extent it is possible to set in motion these inner processes of thinking, feeling, and willing. We find that interest in the subtleties of structuring a lesson has generally waned. Nevertheless, teaching naturally has a temporal structure—but it has been shown that this is basically very simple when the focus is on enabling progress.

This merely formal framework of lessons enables innumerable variations of teaching, depending on the design of the phases. It is so open that it allows for learning progress in different ways and does not prejudge any particular form of teaching. The framework includes four segments:

- In the *opening*, the teacher informs about the topic, the focus, the purposes, and the desired results (you can call it "transparent opening").
- An *introduction to the topic* in most cases is done with input from the teacher, sometimes with conversation. The basal information is provided, and the main points that the students need in order to continue are explained.
- The *learning activities* that follow are essential for learning. They must be introduced and organized. Students should also know what to do if they have difficulties and how to check their own progress.
- *Summing up* usually closes the lesson, and time should be allocated for it. You look together with the students at what has been achieved, where there are open questions, and consequently, what the next steps are.

This cascade of four phases (figure 6.1) is, as said, not a concept to be imposed on the teachers, but follows from the necessities and logics of the lessons under today's conditions. This structure is very open; it corresponds to the real and proven practice of professional teachers, which has stood the test of time and is suitable to allow students to progress.

The elements that make up lessons are discussed in detail and explained with examples in the book *Core Practices of Successful Teachers: Supporting Learning and Managing Instruction* (Fraefel, 2023).

Foundation 3: Practices of Teaching as a Prerequisite

Already toward the end of chapter 2 we talked about practices or core practices. Their importance for successful teaching cannot be overestimated. It is not lesson plans but practices that are the glue of teaching. It is the practices that allow for situational adaptation; they ensure smooth transitions where otherwise discontinuities would occur; it is the practices that allow for unstressed and disciplined improvisation when the

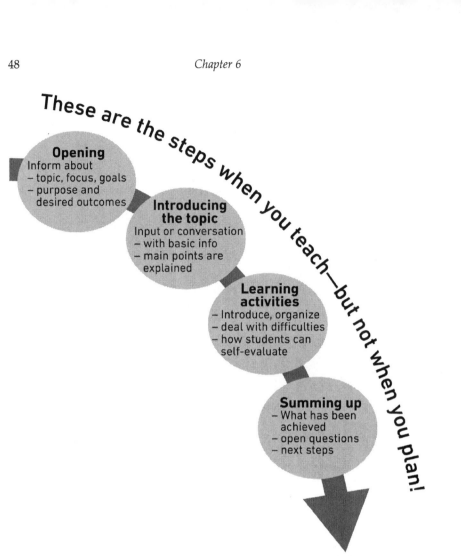

Figure 6.1. The four phases of the course of almost every lesson. *Created by the author*

plan cannot be implemented. However, it cannot be assumed that all teachers have already internalized good practices of teaching, especially preservice teachers.

- Some student teachers therefore stick to their lesson plans; this is associated with the hope that one will have a better handle on teaching even when the unexpected happens. This approach is sometimes encouraged in teacher training. However, situational control through planning is not a sustainable strategy; it does not replace professional practices.

- Or, as mentioned earlier, student teachers overestimate themselves and rely on a few routines without having already internalized the truly supportive and professional practices. The result is amateurish improvisation, as we know.

Acquiring practices

For some teachers, such internalized and flexibly applicable practices are not in place, particularly for less experienced teachers; there is much to learn especially for student teachers. How will one successfully deal with the inherent openness of pedagogical situations (or social situations in general)? By practicing and learning to act appropriately in the situation, that is, by acquiring and internalizing appropriate practices. These are the crucial tools in unplannable situations. They are the prerequisite for smoothly and effectively transforming planning work into concrete lessons in the classroom.

What if the teacher does not yet have these practices? If they have not yet embraced basic patterns of professional teaching? This is a valid objection. Indeed, we are assuming here that certain practices and taken-for-granted things about teaching have already been internalized. Student teachers who have not yet established these practices need different strategies in the training situation. More on this in the book *Core Practices of Successful Teachers: Supporting Learning and Managing Instruction* (Fraefel, in press).

The next chapter of lesson planning in teacher education will show ways in which practices can be acquired and practiced, and how this can be addressed early in the planning process.

What practices? The example of the TeachingWorks program

There continues to be a debate about what the so-called core practices are and how exactly they can be defined. It is clear that certain flexible patterns of action are indispensable for teachers, but it is equally clear that their manifestation can differ from teacher to teacher, without any differences in quality being discernible.

Notwithstanding these considerations, it is useful to have suggestions for a set of core practices, such as the TeachingWorks program, founded by Deborah Ball. It is often cited in the context of core practices. The core practices articulated by TeachingWorks are largely cross-curricular and were originally developed for primary teachers (see box).

According to Ball and Forzani (2009), it is these "high-leverage" practices that form the foundations for accountable teaching; they are used all the time and are critical to helping students learn the things that matter.

According to TeachingWorks, "these practices are used constantly and are critical to helping students learn important content. The high-leverage practices are also central to supporting students' social and emotional development. They are used across subject areas, grade levels, and contexts. They are 'high-leverage' not only because they matter to student learning but because they are basic for advancing skill in teaching." (TeachingWorks, n.d.).

Whether the core or high-leverage practices can be precisely named, and whether there is an exhaustive list to do so, is debatable. However, TeachingWorks is a helpful attempt to name an indispensable core of practices.

The Nineteen "High-Leverage" Practices of the TeachingWorks Program

Only the titles are reproduced here. For detailed descriptions of the practices see https://www.teachingworks.org/high-leverage-practices (retrieved April 17, 2023).

1. Leading a group discussion
2. Explaining and modeling content
3. Eliciting and interpreting individual students' thinking
4. Attending to patterns of student thinking
5. Implementing norms and routines for discourse
6. Coordinating and adjusting instruction
7. Establishing and maintaining community expectations
8. Implementing organizational routines
9. Setting up and managing small group work
10. Building respectful relationships
11. Communicating with families
12. Learning about students
13. Setting learning goals
14. Designing single lessons and sequences of lessons
15. Checking student understanding
16. Selecting and designing assessments
17. Interpreting student work
18. Providing feedback to students
19. Analyzing instruction for the purpose of improving it

NOT A LESSON PLAN BUT A STRINGENT STRATEGY

The goal of lesson planning is not a lesson plan, but student learning. The following considerations and recommendations therefore do not result in a planning template, of which there are known to be numerous in circulation, and which foster the illusion that planning is done with a fully completed lesson plan.

Everyone is familiar with these templates, often in tabular form and prefaced with notes of all possible preliminary considerations. The tabular overviews usually break down the surface structure of the lesson—sequence, teacher and student activities, time management, materials, and so on. Here we present a leaner way of planning lessons.

Again: Backward Planning

So, what does backward planning mean for the particular lesson? It means getting serious about reversing the direction of planning and starting with the desired results. Let's look again at figure 6.1: the progression of the lesson begins with an opening, followed by introduction and learning activities, and ending with a summing up of what has been learned. At this final phase of the lesson, it is expected that the goals have been met, that what is desired has been learned, and this is where planning must start.

Defining desired results (building on the unit planning and the students' present situation)

The teacher gets clear on what progress students are expected to make. These expected results are reflected in the assessment tasks already designed in unit planning. The assessment tasks are, in a sense, the hinge between unit planning and lesson planning. Through the assessment tasks (which are also learning tasks), the teacher sees what the students are expected to know and be able to do at the end.

Now the teacher should *adjust the expected results to the actual possibilities*. How much is possible? Is there enough time to do it? And where do the students stand? Are they thirsty for new challenges or do they continue to struggle? In short, the teacher will portion the expected outcomes so that they can realistically be achieved in this lesson, and that's done by selecting the appropriate tasks to master.

By the way, the lesson does not have to end with a test. Mostly, this would be a waste of time just to find out if the students have achieved the expected results, and it only makes the students nervous. Responsive teachers diagnose progress and difficulties already during the lesson and can also react immediately. All that matters is that the teacher learns where the students are now, what they have learned, where there are gaps, where more time is needed or questions need to be answered, and so on. With a test at the end of the lesson it is different: however it turns out, it would be too late to do anything about it. A formative short test is rarely the best solution. However, sooner or later, usually toward the end of a unit, there will be a summative and often graded assessment, and the students will be well prepared for this, because they know the objectives and the tasks they are expected to cope with.

Preparing learning activities

Students, as we know, learn little from just listening. When they are actively engaged with tasks, problems, challenges, they learn best. So, the next step is to plan these learning activities—that is, to plan tasks and assignments. After all, the foundation has already been laid in unit planning.

Preparing an introduction to the topic

Now another step back. What do students need to engage meaningfully and productively with the tasks? The teacher needs to provide some basic information and basic explanations so that students can get started with the learning activities. Sometimes a classroom discussion might also be appropriate for this purpose.

Preparing a transparent opening

All of these teacher considerations are still completely unknown to the students. Therefore, it is important that the teacher plans a transparent opening so that everyone understands what today is about being on the same page.

Let's summarize: the key is now to *reverse the course of the lesson when planning*. The actual lesson is linear—from opening to summing up (see figure 6.1). But the planning is done in reverse, starting with what is to be achieved at the end (figure 6.2), and these desired results are expressed in tasks (assessment tasks that can be learning tasks at the same time).

Lesson plan: Just a simple outline—succinct and expedient, without anything self-evident

Traditional lesson templates often want too much. You can't cram everything into a tabular lesson plan, because neither the self-evident nor the unpredictable need to be recorded in writing. In fact, the form in which

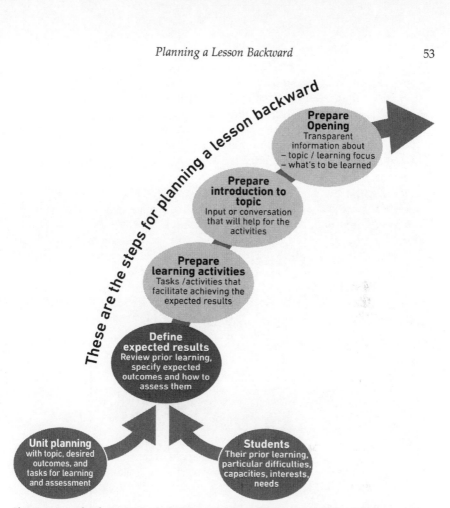

Figure 6.2. The four steps of planning a lesson backward, starting with the expected results, which are specified in the form of tasks. *Created by the author*

the teacher takes notes is largely irrelevant. They can be recorded on cards or in the usual tabular format. for example, in the form of one or more postcard-sized pieces of paper, summarizing the approximate course of the lesson and containing a few points that the teacher should not forget; that's sufficient. More importantly, the notes should be concise and allow for flexible navigation through the lesson.

The two rules of thumb are:

- **Note all important points**—what is particularly important today, what is important for learning progress, what must not be forgotten.
- **Leave out everything that is self-evident**, for example, most of the explanations about the social setting, the media, and so forth, because they are clear or arise casually, possibly during the input or the

classroom discussion. So why write down what is self-evident and already internalized (in the form of professional practices)? Demanding this would only anger the teachers.

This outline is, of course, supplemented by the necessary *materials* (documents of all kinds, tasks, technical equipment). What does *not* need to be written down, on the other hand, is the knowledge and practices already internalized by the teacher. Why write down what is clear anyway?

Such a lesson plan with only the stepping stones of the lesson, so to speak—we mentioned it earlier—gives teachers both a *solid structure and a great deal of openness in teaching*; the planning strategy does not force teachers to follow a rigid step-by-step pattern. If things turn out differently than expected, teachers can make ad hoc adjustments—assuming they have the basic knowledge and a few practices to respond quickly.

Again, flexible and adaptive teaching can only be mastered if the materials from the unit's overarching planning are available, and the teacher has sound practices.

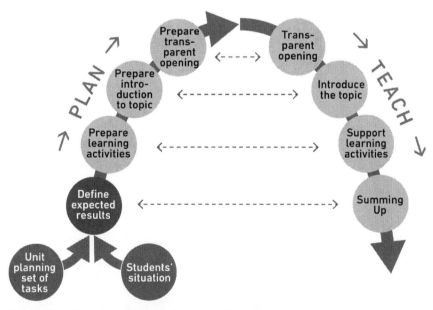

Figure 6.3. Overview of lesson planning and teaching: planning steps backward starting from the end, then teaching and enacting forward. *Created by the author*

Ensuring flexibility

A planning template tempts to plan in a linear fashion, in other words, to work through the phases at the planned pace. But student-centered planning is always flexible planning. It's analogous to a card game in which the player has a good hand and plays as needed the card that is most purposeful. The pace is set by the students' learning progress, not the lesson plan. Even in forty-minute lessons, adaptivity is possible and necessary; indeed, it is a quality feature of a lesson that wants to do right by its students.

Well, how can this be done? If necessary, *each phase can be divided, repeated, and rearranged,* except for the opening of the lesson, which is of course at the beginning. For example:

- **Repetition:** Input, learning activities, and summing up can be run through twice.
- **Interruptions:** Additional input is given during the activity phase.
- **Review of the current state:** These can help to make a preliminary point about what has already been achieved.
- **Classroom discussions:** Ad hoc scheduled exchange in the whole class.

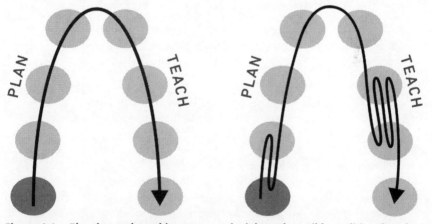

Figure 6.4. Planning and teaching steps—principle and possible realities (based on figure 6.3). *Created by the author*

CONCLUSION

For lean and efficient planning, it is advisable to rethink and change some habits. In-service teachers don't need to use elaborate templates from teacher education to plan professionally; they just need to stick to a few obvious principles. Those who take backward planning seriously can limit the effort and make the work more substantial. Planning is focused on what matters: supporting *all* learners' progress as best as possible.

ACTIVITIES AND SUGGESTIONS

STARTING FROM THE END: IT IS UNFAMILIAR AND NEEDS TO BE PRACTICED

This Point Is Really Important

Do some practicing of thinking from the end, in other words, planning backward. It is an effort, but it is worth it. The payoff for you and the learners is huge, but you'll have to rewire a few connections in your head. And whenever possible, do it together with peers.

What You Need to Do to Acquire This Practice

Follow this instruction step by step and do it several times. You will quickly notice the effect on yourself. Of course, it's best to do it with lessons you'll actually be doing.

1. **Imagine a lesson**
   - Take a lesson on a topic you will teach next, but if that is not possible, then you can also plan a lesson on reserve for later, preferably on a topic you have taught before.
   - Then write down in very few keywords what it is about.
2. **Design the assessment (this is the core step!)**
   Now plan in as much detail as possible how you would check what progress students have made on that topic by designing tasks that students would have to solve at the end of the lesson. The guiding idea is: if all students do well on this assessment, I'm happy.
3. **Check the quality of your assessment**
   Once you have put the tasks together, ask yourself again:
   - Can the students really show with these tasks what they have learned?

- Or are the tasks too mundane, or perhaps too focused on reproduction of knowledge or on rote memorization?
- Or do the tasks ask something that is not at the core of the topic at all?

Be self-critical and discard or change the tasks if they do not meet these criteria. A simple way to check the quality of the tasks:
- Imagine that a student might already solve all your tasks at the beginning of the lesson. Could you just as well let that student leave the class, since they already understand everything? If you can answer yes, the tasks are perfect.

4. **Observe the desirable side effects of designing tasks**
   If you do this seriously, you will find that in designing the tasks you have
   - sharpened the objectives, because you need to know what you want to achieve with the tasks; and
   - deepened the content again, because only with a deep understanding of the topic can you design meaningful tasks.

5. **Design the lesson**
   - *Only now* do you consider how you need to design the lesson so that as many of the students as possible can master as many of the tasks as possible at the end.
   - Outline in a few keywords how you would do this. Of course, you can use the tasks you have just designed.
   - At the beginning of the lesson, you will be able to use the tasks to inform the students exactly what they have to learn.

6. **Repeat from the start**
   Repeat this exercise a few times, and of course with topics that you can use later. This will help you appreciate the benefits of planning as such.

7

⊗

Planning Lessons by and with Student Teachers

STUDENT TEACHERS PLAN DIFFERENTLY

Student teachers inevitably plan differently because they have had few opportunities to acquire consolidated practices that they have already internalized and that facilitate flexible and adaptive teaching. In teacher education, they have a unique and ideal learning environment for doing so. But given the emphasis on planning in teacher education, a preliminary remark is unavoidable.

All professionals who train student teachers have an opinion about planning, have their favorite theoretical references, preferences, and conventions. Often, a lot of emphasis is placed on the appropriate vocabulary and the use of certain schemes. Therefore, the following suggestions should always be read with the caveat of compatibility with institutional guidelines.

The Myth of the Perfect Lesson and the Problem of Overwhelming the Student Teachers

Teaching during teacher education has a very important function: *professional practices that student teachers do not yet possess must first be formed* to ultimately enable smooth and successful teaching. It is imperative that these practices be developed in teacher education, because it would be irresponsible to focus on them only at the beginning of one's career—most teachers are overwhelmed with this challenge when they enter the profession, and most importantly, students suffer.

This means that student teachers do not need to pretend to be experienced teachers—they simply lack the professional practices to do so. Student teachers may want to design entire lessons on their own to make sure they are capable of doing so, and this may even work—but they are inevitably focused on surface structure, on the "functioning" of what is visible. Therefore, student teachers should not be overburdened and expected to do everything right away: to be there entirely for the learners *and* to design professional lessons for all learners on their own that are conducive to learning *and* to improve their own practices at the same time. This is simply too much for beginners.

But paradoxically, many student teachers and even cooperating teachers disagree with this view. All too quickly, they think they now know how to teach. This may be true at best on a visual level, but it is not enough to keep an eye on the learning and development of all students, to provide them with optimal support and encouragement, and even to help them overcome a crisis from time to time.

In most cases, teacher education nevertheless adheres to planning and delivering stand-alone lessons as the "standard format." Since the lesson is the dominant formal framework in professional reality, it is mostly unquestioned in teacher education when the "lesson" is the preferred form of practice and is repetitively practiced over and over again. The importance of the lesson is exaggerated, its perfect execution is sometimes elevated to a sophisticated work of art, and teacher trainers and student teachers at times hone the best possible staging with perseverance.

But this misses the real necessities, because everyone knows: the lesson that promotes learning is complex and presents an overload situation. Therefore, student teachers would need to be able to have learning experiences in manageable, less complex situations.

How exactly should complexity be reduced in teacher education? The most common strategy in teacher education to reduce complexity is to build a support system around teaching to prevent failure, which is done with three measures:

- Traditionally, through accurate planning, to get a handle on all contingencies
- Traditionally, through the presence of professionals to ensure a low-disturbance environment
- Traditionally, in reflective postlesson conferences in order to draw conclusions

This support system helps student teachers learn to organize lessons at the surface level, but it provides limited training opportunities for building professional practices that truly serve *all* students; in other words, student teachers' learning opportunities to do so are very limited.

The Alternative: Training Professional Practices Instead of Delivering Lessons

The alternative is that student teachers need more space to practice, revise, and improve their practices over and over again, but they *do not have to be solely responsible* for making the lessons work. This fundamentally changes the focus of internships and practicums.

The Two Modes

Let's contrast the traditional mode and the core-practices mode:

- In the *traditional mode*, the focus is on delivering whole lessons. If student teachers get to learn practices at all, it tends to be incidental. In short:
  Whole-lesson practice → incidental training in core practices at best.
- In the *core-practices mode*, on the other hand, the emphasis is on training and practicing core practices. Through this, student teachers acquire knowledge and skills to master adaptive and effective teaching. In short:
  Focusing core practices → acquiring mastery of adaptive and effective teaching.

The transition to the core-practices mode also requires a change in thinking on the part of teacher educators and cooperating teachers: the silver bullet of the practicum is thus not to learn well-organized and smooth lessons; rather, the emphasis is on very specific areas—practices—of professional action in which student teachers are to become "professionals." With the rehearsal of such flexible components, the building blocks of lessons, they are well prepared to teach their own classes in a learner-focused and adaptive manner.

Co-teaching in Teacher Education: A Unique Learning Opportunity

Rehearsing practices rather than delivering lessons: teacher education practicums and internships easily allow for such a setting; indeed, they are predestined for it, because there is always an experienced teacher and usually other student teachers as well. This is a good thing, because student teachers could not master this challenge alone.

That's why co-teaching is essential to relieve student teachers of the abundance of simultaneous tasks in the classroom. They can concentrate on one thing, really learn it, and leave everything else to their colleagues for the time being. In addition, students also benefit from the setting with multiple teachers who have thoroughly prepared for their subtask. Co-planning is closely related to co-teaching and has been theoretically, empirically, and conceptually deepened since the turn of the millennium (e.g., Guise et al., 2017; Murphy & Scantlebury, 2010; West & Staub, 2003).

Seen in this light, student teachers are largely relieved of "delivering lessons," but are given *two new tasks* in co-teaching: (1) supporting the learners, and (2) rehearsing their core practices to become more professional.

Take a look at figure 7.1, which shows the principle of the cyclic process in a practicum: The outer circle represents what student teachers and cooperating teachers do together. The inner circle names everything student teachers can and should do on their own.

The decisive factor is *joint planning (co-planning)* on the left side of the figure. Certainly not all parts of the planning need to be done together, which would be overkill. For example, the deeper understanding of learning tasks and the underlying content can be mastered by student teachers alone. Practical things like providing materials and writing down the outline can also be done by student teachers themselves. However, the *fundamental as well as strategic decisions* are always discussed and made jointly by student teachers and cooperating teachers.

Co-planning is unbreakably linked to *co-teaching* (on the right side of figure 7.1), which in turn requires learning on two levels: student learning on the one hand, and student teacher learning in terms of practices on the other; we'll get into that in a moment. The postlesson conference takes up a small amount of time and is more of a debriefing: briefly summarizing where everyone stands and what the next steps are for the class and the student teachers. This is where the planning process comes full circle, starting again with the common question, what to do based on the experiences of the last lesson, what goals and focus to set: on the one hand for the students, but on the other hand also for the student teachers.

Strong focus on flexibility in co-teaching: Potentiation of student teachers' progress

How can student teachers learn flexibility as a crucial feature of instruction that promotes learning? Co-planning and co-teaching provide a perfect training ground. Everything is easier in pairs (or threes). Co-teaching relieves student teachers of the pressure to demonstrate lessons that work on the surface, because in co-teaching, a team of at least two adults is teaching and sharing responsibility for the lesson.

Adults as well as students can become accustomed to co-teaching very quickly, as all experience and numerous studies on co-teaching show (e.g., Guise et al., 2017; Rabin, 2020); the sometimes exam-like tension

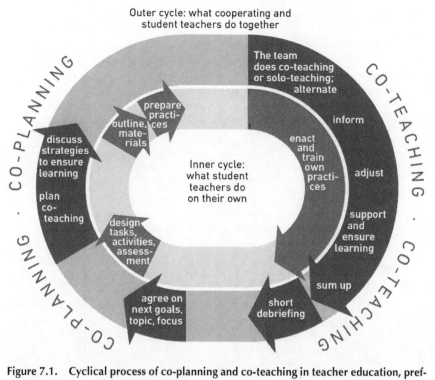

Outer cycle: what cooperating and
student teachers do together

CO-PLANNING · CO-PLANNING

CO-TEACHING · CO-TEACHING

The team
does co-teaching
or solo-teaching;
alternate

inform

enact
and
train
own
practi-
ces

adjust

support
and
ensure
learning

sum up

short
debriefing

agree on
next goals,
topic, focus

design
tasks,
activities,
assess-
ment

plan
co-
teaching

discuss
strategies
to ensure
learning

prepare
practi-
ces

outline,
mate-
rials

Inner cycle:
what student
teachers do
on their own

Figure 7.1. Cyclical process of co-planning and co-teaching in teacher education, preferably with two student teachers and one cooperating teacher. *Created by the author*

when student teachers demonstrate lessons gives way to an atmosphere of natural cooperation.

Those who co-teach can always pause briefly to consider whether this is the right way to go and what is next to move learners forward. A brief exchange of a few seconds can clarify what comes next and who does what. The elements prepared—opening, input, conversation, activities, and so forth—can be adjusted, interrupted, shifted, or repeated as the situation requires. Collaborative decisions to change the plan are better founded if they are supported by two or three teachers; wrong decisions and idle time are less likely.

Adaptive design in practicums and internships strengthens the conscious perception of what is happening in the classroom. A big advantage: corrections are made immediately, and mistakes are not just pointed out only after the fact in the postlesson conference. With every intermediate decision about how to proceed, learning is involved. Thus, co-planning and co-teaching obviously potentiate the learning effect for the student teachers.

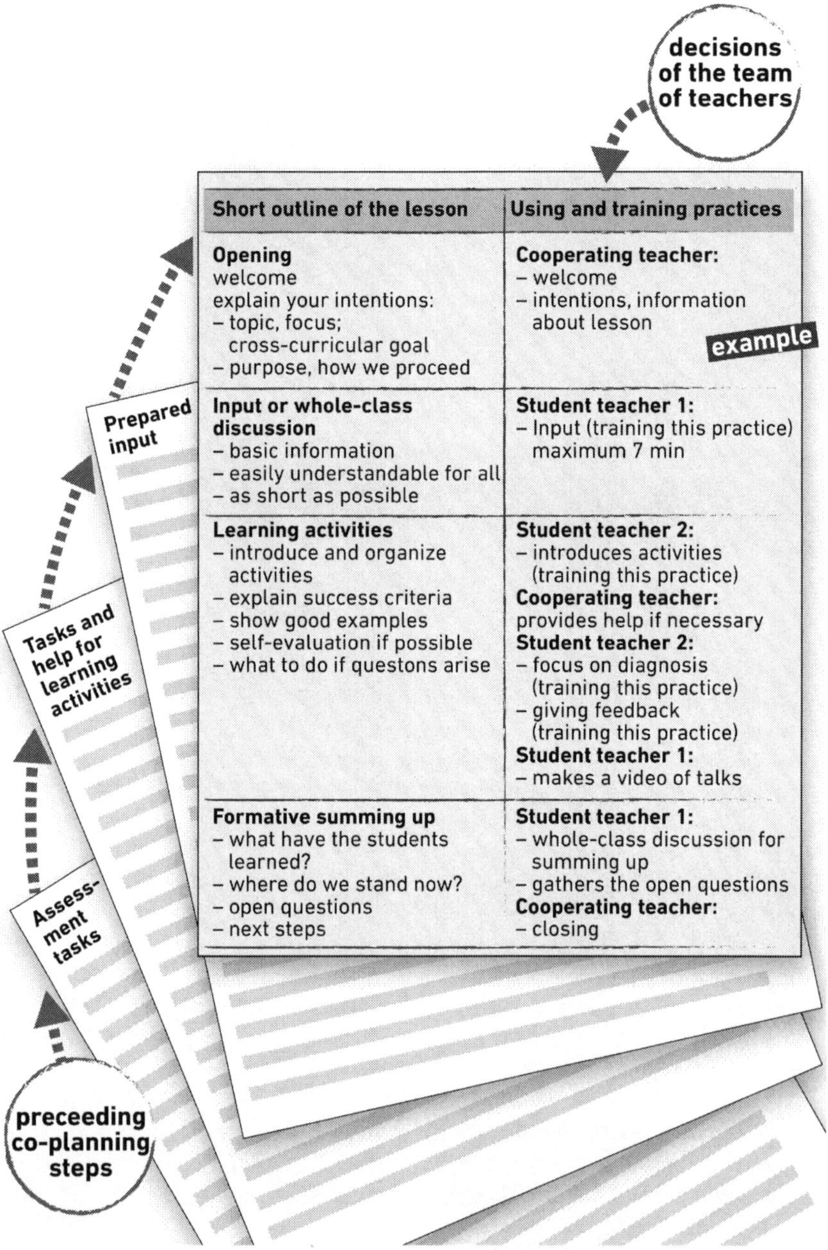

decisions of the team of teachers

Short outline of the lesson	Using and training practices

Opening
welcome
explain your intentions:
– topic, focus;
   cross-curricular goal
– purpose, how we proceed
	Cooperating teacher:
	– welcome
	– intentions, information
	   about lesson
	
	example

Input or whole-class discussion – basic information – easily understandable for all – as short as possible	**Student teacher 1:** – Input (training this practice) maximum 7 min

Learning activities
– introduce and organize
   activities
– explain success criteria
– show good examples
– self-evaluation if possible
– what to do if questons arise
	Student teacher 2:
	– introduces activities
	   (training this practice)
	Cooperating teacher:
	provides help if necessary
	Student teacher 2:
	– focus on diagnosis
	   (training this practice)
	– giving feedback
	   (training this practice)
	Student teacher 1:
	– makes a video of talks

Formative summing up
– what have the students
   learned?
– where do we stand now?
– open questions
– next steps
	Student teacher 1:
	– whole-class discussion for
	   summing up
	– gathers the open questions
	Cooperating teacher:
	– closing

Prepared input

Tasks and help for learning activities

Assessment tasks

preceeding co-planning steps

Figure 7.2.   Structure of a written outline for a lesson in co-teaching. *Created by the author*

How Should Student Teachers' Lesson Outlines Be Written Down?

We may assume that teacher education has an interest in providing planning routines for later professional practice that will actually be used. But to do that, the planning routines need to be boiled down to the essentials. Components that are experienced as meaningless formalisms during teacher education are quite likely to generate resistance to formalized planning.

- Nevertheless, *everyone wants guidelines for planning*—student teachers, teachers, and teacher educators—so that the designs are manageable, do not diverge in grotesque ways, and remain comprehensible to others.
- *And the bar must be set high.* The quality and coherence of learning activities and inputs is a priority; poor teaching is not justifiable in terms of professional ethics.
- And, as discussed earlier, *not every idea needs to be spelled out* in the lesson plan, because in backward planning, central aspects (goals, coherence) are implicitly included. That must be enough.
- If a teacher educator or cooperating teacher wants to understand in more depth the reasoning involved in planning, a *conversation* seems more appropriate.

Figure 7.2 shows what should suffice for an outline. Attached in each case are the materials (tasks, notes for input, etc., some also digital, e.g., presentations, pictures).

Also plan for co-teaching and the practices to be used and trained!

We looked at a simple way to take notes for a lesson in the last chapter: an outline of key points, plus additional materials as needed. It is also true in co-teaching that things should be kept simple. The fact that two to three people are now involved does not change this. But it's not just about student teaching, it's also about *student teacher learning*. Therefore, an outline must also capture these learning processes of the prospective teachers. Therefore, a second column describes team collaboration and student teacher learning activities (cf. figures 7.2 and 7.3):

1. In the first column, there is a short lesson outline, jointly prepared along the phases, with some keywords.
2. In the second column, the responsibilities for each phase are added, as well as indications on which practices the student teachers will work.

The materials needed, especially for the activity phase—tasks, assignments, documentation for them, suggested solutions, and so on—are simply attached.

And Do Student Teachers Learn to Deliver Entire Lessons on Their Own? Of Course They Do

It is really surprising that this question comes up again and again, when there is talk of co-teaching in teacher education. Well, the benefits of

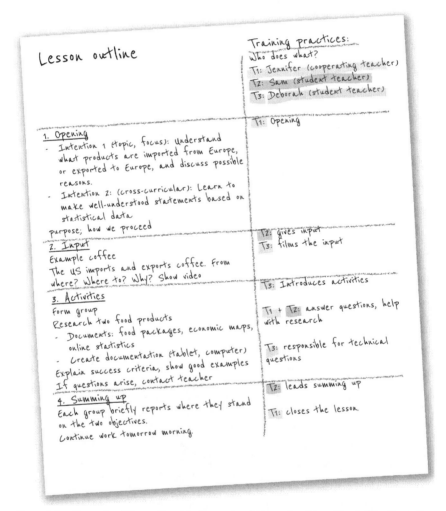

Figure 7.3.   Example of the outline of a lesson taught in co-teaching. *Created by the author*

systematic co-teaching in placements are increasingly recognized. But student teachers are driven by an understandable urge to be able to teach on their own and to gain certainty about their own instructional design and classroom management skills.

Surprisingly and paradoxically, student teachers learn to teach alone much better through co-teaching and even more thoroughly because they gain confidence in many particular practices and are not overly preoccupied with ensuring the flow of the lesson.

While being cautious about comparisons, one can take a look at other professions where people work only as a team for a long time until someone finally takes over sole responsibility: lawyers, pilots, surgeons, therapists, cooks, engineers, and so on. Hardly any profession expects its young people to have to cope with the professional demands alone right from the start; at the end of a long learning period, however, things go surprisingly easily, even when finally acting alone—precisely because the introduction to the professional activities was so gentle.

The same can be said for the profession of teaching. Student teachers can train, vary, optimize their individual practices over many years. The sum of the practices will readily allow them to shape a professional classroom on their own.

ACTIVITIES AND SUGGESTIONS

MAKE ARRANGEMENTS WITH THE TEACHER IN WHOSE CLASS YOU ARE DOING YOUR PRACTICUM OR INTERNSHIP

Sometimes little room for training of practices

Depending on the institution and the prevailing traditions, internships or practicums are organized differently and the assignments of the school of education to the cooperating teachers vary greatly. In many cases, student teachers also have to fulfill assignments from their school of education and report on them after the field experience. This makes internships cumbersome and leaves little room for practicing one's own practices. So, what to do?

1. **Have an early conversation with the cooperating teacher**—Take time before the practicum to talk with the cooperating teacher about the nature of the collaboration. Cooperating teachers cannot know what is important to you at this time and what practices you want to progress in unless you tell them.

2. **Make arrangements with the cooperating teacher**—It is definitely advisable to clarify at least the following points before the practicum or internship:
   - Are we setting intentions or goals for a unit and lessons together?
   - Can I discuss what I have planned with the cooperating teacher in advance? Will I get critical feedback on my planning outline before I teach?
   - Is the cooperating teacher willing to teach together with me?
   - Can we share classroom activities between us so that I can focus on one practice?
   - If the cooperating teacher is not familiar with backward planning, are they willing to try it out with me and embark on this adventure?
   - When training practices, occasional failure is inevitable. Does this affect the *evaluation* of the practicum?
3. **Keep track of what is important to you at the moment**—Write down what would be important to you right now in the above points if you were to start a practicum or an internship next. In other words: How do you envision your ideal working relationship with the cooperating teacher?

8

~∞~

What Goals for Units?
What Expected Results?
What Tasks?

Society commits young people to learning and expresses it in terms of intentions, goals, and standards; teachers carry the goals to the children and young people. Thus, teaching is always intentional, which is not necessarily the case when we learn something in everyday life.

School is essentially about expectations of progress and achievement. Those who have expectations and set standards want them to be met, and so formative and summative assessment is also an essential part of school. This chapter delves into these issues, which have been addressed occasionally before.

MOSTLY, TEACHERS WANT TO TEACH
RATHER THAN THINK ABOUT GOALS

What fascinates teachers about their own profession is teaching and dealing with children and young people. This is where they mostly derive the satisfaction and recognition they deserve. Planning and preparation are also mostly geared toward helping teachers master the visible process of teaching.

In contrast, goal setting is not an activity for which teachers receive a "reward"; indeed, often an uninvolved observer or the learners do not even notice whether goals have been set at all, since teaching can also flow along aimlessly.

And yet, it is precisely the strategy that is developed prior to the action that is often decisive for success, as in the case of pilots who work through checklists and study weather forecasts and flight routes, or surgeons who immerse themselves in medical records, plan the operations with their team, and so on. The fatal thing about the teaching profession is that professional errors are often not immediately apparent, unlike those of a pilot or surgeon, for example. Nevertheless, this lack of a strategy has a long-term effect, even if rarely instantly resulting in a catastrophe visible to all: the progress of the students will be slower or stagnant, the confusion greater, the interest flagging. It's a silent, often unnoticed disaster.

The importance of goals is undisputed; it is only the long-winded procedures of goal setting that cause discomfort. And yes, for beginning teachers, the whole complex of goals and goal setting is often burdensome. But don't worry, here we show a straightforward, understandable, and attractive way to arrive at clear intentions.

WHAT WE ALREADY KNOW

1. Teachers Must Want Something (Which Is Always to Advance the Students)

Real intentions cannot be derived schematically, because intentions are expressions of the *will to achieve something*. It is a very personal thing. Intentions are the answer to the question "Where are we going?" To put it pointedly, "doing something" is not enough; a teacher must "*want* something." The teacher develops the will to make a difference in each student; students should learn and understand, they should grow and make progress, they should overcome dry spells and have a sense of success.

2. There Are Always Goals—but Preferably Transparent Ones Rather Than Hidden Ones

For example, a teacher can pretend that the goals are not important, but the students interpret very accurately what implicit goals the teacher sets, because they have enough time to study the teacher's unspoken preferences. for example, memorize pure factual knowledge, sit still, pretend interest (even in boring topics). What students are expected to do in an unspoken way is also known as the "hidden curriculum." Hidden expectations poison the learning atmosphere. Therefore, there are only advantages to speaking openly and understandably about where the journey is going and how.

3. From Forward Planning to Backward Planning

Tyler (1949) proposed a forward planning sequencing as early as the mid-twentieth century that has strongly influenced the planning behavior of many teachers ever since:

Goals → Activities → Lesson Design → Assessment

Since the adoption of standards and the greater focus on testing, a shift in the scheme has been proposed on various occasions (e.g., Drost & Levine, 2015):

Standards → Goals → Assessment → Lesson Design

Wiggins and McTighe (2011), who have most intensively driven the reverse planning process, name the elements slightly differently, but in principle it amounts to the same thing:

Desired Results → Evidence → Learning Plan

By the way, it seems like a good idea that Wiggins and McTighe often replace the well-worn words "goals" and "objectives" with "expected results" or "desired results." This basically means the same thing, but the intent and purpose of the goals is much clearer with this choice of words. This wording is also used several times here.

4. Objectives Materialize in the Tasks, the Currency of Learning in School

Detailed objectives do not have to be formulated; those schematic rules are exhausting and formalistic (e.g., use certain verbs like "can show," "can summarize," "is able to perform"). It is the *tasks* that show us what the goals, that is, the desired results, are.

Beware, trap!

Everything that has been said so far about tasks may come to nothing if you take on any tasks from a third party without thinking. After all, there are thousands of suggestions on activities for any topic. Use them, but get rid of all the ones that do not address exactly what you think is important. More about this later.

Example: "Read this blog post and summarize it in about one hundred words so that classmates who don't know the post will get the most important information in a way that is easy to read and understand." What the teacher thinks should be achieved is expressed by this task. Such a task eliminates the need for cumbersome goal-setting prose that probably no one will ever read anyway. You can save this duplicate work.

Tasks are the linchpin of learning in school, its currency. Not only do they clarify the goals and the success criteria that have been set, but they require activity (which is essential for learning), and they are the means by which desired results are monitored.

THE PRACTICE OF ALIGNING UNIT INTENTIONS WITH STANDARDS

In short, this is about a pragmatic way for teachers to deal with given requirements. We do not engage in nuanced discussions, nor do we provide a template for how to break down standards in a formalistic way. So, it is about a practice of goal setting that is consistent with standards. This practice needs to be rehearsed and adopted.

The Unit Is the Entry Point

Things can be made very complicated—to get from the most general standards to concrete objectives in the classroom, one can insert many intermediate steps, which, moreover, can vary by country, state, school, grade level, and subject. However, it is obvious that teachers set their intentions at the *unit level* (units as a series of lessons on a topic). This is the time period they are overlooking for concrete planning, and this is relevant in this context.

We are not addressing here the following distinctions, which, by the way, are not completely separable, nor are they always used with exactly the same meaning:

- The curriculum describes the structure and timeline of all objectives on a subject.
- The syllabus outlines goals, content, and assessments in a subject.
- In schemes of work, a longer period of time in a subject is preplanned (e.g., half a year).

Depending on the local conditions, the curriculum, the syllabus, and the scheme of work are given (by superiors, by textbooks, etc.) or they are worked out in teams, or they are designed by the teachers themselves. Of course, all of this can be used if it serves the cause. However, we leave aside how these levels are worked out and focus entirely on finding *standards-based goals for units*.

Standards—Essential Guidelines for Teaching

If employers set guidelines for what they want employees to do, that's their right. The same applies if they want to check whether the requirements have been met. As far as schools are concerned, these guidelines are now set as standards, albeit sometimes with differences from state to state, from school to school.

The guidelines for teachers have a long history. They have always been accompanied by controversy and even polemics as different philosophies, beliefs, and interests collide. In addition, the logic of the standards is often not directly apparent, and the logic of the authors' conscientious thinking is sometimes not immediately apparent to teachers.

It is not necessary for us to go into details here, but nonetheless it is worth mentioning the questions that have repeatedly preoccupied the developers of standards:

- Should students acquire knowledge first and foremost? What kind of knowledge? Should content be stated, or goals defined? What skills should students acquire?
- Is it about the introduction to our common culture, or about the preparation for professional life, or about the personal development of the students? Or all of it?
- How detailed should objectives be, and how much scope for decision-making do teachers have?
- Should only minimum requirements or the ideally desired requirements be defined?
- Should it also be specified *how* the goals or standards are to be achieved? (see Gamson et al., 2019).

These are basically very important questions, some of which go to the heart of school and the teaching profession, and on which most teachers have formed opinions. Be that as it may, the reality for teachers is that they have to find a way to meet the standards, and they can take advantage of the prior work done by education experts. Standards don't just constrain; they also relieve teachers of difficult decisions and are a useful planning resource.

Referring to Standards, Using the Freedoms

Again, we need to clarify a *potential misunderstanding* here: goals and activities *cannot be derived formalistically from standards*. Standards are an important guideline, perhaps an inspiration, but they are not prescriptive. *It takes responsible teachers* to decide on intentions and flesh them out to the tasks.

Teachers can and must—within the broad bounds of the standards—take their liberties with unit planning. Sometimes a certain topic is a priority, sometimes a certain skill. The teacher's own preferences and special capabilities may also be incorporated. After all, it is obvious that lessons become more interesting, more credible, and more authentic when students sense that the teacher is engaged in them with joy and commitment.

Let us remember the simple scheme of how planning works in principle. We have discussed the steps leading to unit planning (figure 5.1). In the following pages, we are focusing in particular on the first steps, namely, how to *decide on topic and desired outcomes*.

FURTHER INFORMATION AND RESOURCES

THIS IS HOW YOU FIND COHERENT TOPICS AND INTENTIONS (= DESIRED RESULTS) FOR UNITS: A VERY SHORT INTRODUCTION

These four simple steps should lead to clear and authentic topics and intentions of units of several lessons. Immediately following this box are suggestions for how you can practice finding topics and intentions.

1. *Review the Standards (or Other Resources, Such as Curricula, Schemes of Work Already Worked Out, Etc.)*

   - Narrow down roughly what domain it is in.
   - Review these standards (or other directives) to get an overview of what is required. This is a little easier these days because many standards are aligned across the country. Teachers no longer have to navigate the jungle of numerous local specifications as much.
   - Put the standards in context—make sure you know what is presupposed and what is likely to follow.
   - Just do it, even if you're not very motivated. While you are dealing with standards and intentions, imagine your students—it helps keep you grounded.

2. Make Your Selection

You may be overwhelmed and confused by the abundance of standards. Therefore, you should make a reasonable choice as soon as possible and focus on a few points. Proceed like this:

- You now have an overview of the general guidelines as well as the specific ones for your subject and grade level. From the mandatory topics, choose one that is reasonable in scope and fits roughly into one unit; just leave all the rest aside for now. "Topic" in the broader sense means not only an area of knowledge, but also skills, cross-curricular aspects, higher-level requirements, and so on.
- A common practice in narrowing standards might be the simple trick of focusing on nouns and verbs: nouns denote content (what students need to know); verbs denote skills (what students need to be able to do).
- If you have a greater freedom of decision and can set important topics or aspects yourself, then use the freedom as long as it is compatible with what is given.

3. Reflect on Your Vision (You Can Reflect on It Anywhere—While Jogging, on the Sofa, or Wherever)

Now you as a person come into play—your commitment, your knowledge, your interests, your urge to convey important things. Be inspired by the richness of the goal variations on the following pages!

- Sound out the potential of the topic to develop "big ideas"— interesting, broader ideas that get students thinking, discussing, and researching. Big ideas are phenomena or questions or events that immediately spark interest and have something larger underlying them—for example, a law of nature, a historical context, or a previously unrecognized regularity. Big ideas are door openers for thinking and discovering deeper connections. If you are fascinated by them yourself, there is a good chance that you will be able to engage your students in this journey of discovery. But it takes some practice to implement this attractive approach, as Windschitl et al. (2012) state: "Beginning teachers, however, are not skilled at identifying such [big] ideas. They typically use curriculum topics and materials uncritically to choose goals for student learning. . . . We found that many of our novices, even with curriculum in hand, could not identify big ideas to teach" (p. 888).

- *Find out for yourself what the purpose*, meaning, and relevance of this topic are (if you don't see the purpose and relevance yourself, you will hardly be able to convey the topic).
- Develop a vision in your mind's eye of *where the students will be at the end of the unit*: what they know, what they can do, how they look at and judge things, how they talk about them, how they tackle analogous problems unabashedly, and so forth.
- Imagine for yourself this final state of the students and the class in the broad strokes (not in the small details).
- The topic will evolve; some things you will leave out, things important in your view will be added or given a special emphasis, until you have a coherent idea, and you can say, "Yes, if we're at this point after four weeks, I'll be happy!"

4. *Specify Your Intentions (What You Expect as a Result)*

- Now specify your intentions (because a topic alone is not an intention). For the whole unit, put into words what you have previously "visioned." Write it down as you wish, but in unsophisticated language that students could understand immediately. Make sure that nothing gets lost and that the skills, generic goals, and more ambitious intentions do not fall by the wayside.
- This need not be detailed, but rather give an overall impression of what the intentions are. Later, this step will also take the form of concrete tasks, which we know are a manifestation of the intentions, and long lists of objectives will be unnecessary.

Note: When it comes to planning the one specific lesson, you will once again sharpen the topic and your intentions and then adjust them to your students. However, this is not necessary yet when planning a unit.

ACTIVITIES AND SUGGESTIONS

PRACTICE FINDING THE TOPIC AND THE INTENTIONS WITH AN EXAMPLE (BASED ON STANDARDS)

You will need two resources for this activity: the standards (or similar guidelines) and your own well-reasoned intuition. We follow the four steps in the previous box and provide an example. You, in turn, do the analogous steps with your own example of an area with which you are somewhat familiar or which you will be teaching yourself in the near future.

1. Review the Standards

Narrow down roughly what domain it is in and get an overview.

Our example:

- Grade 4, English Language Arts
- Writing
- Standards: Common Core State Standards
- We skim the standards and scroll back to see what has already been covered in writing (or remember what has already been done with the class on it).

Your example:

2. Make Your Selection

Choose an approximate topic area suitable for planning a unit.

Our example:

We choose this standard:
- "Write informative/explanatory texts to examine a topic and convey ideas and information clearly." (CCSSO, 2010, p. 20)
- We are looking at samples of student writing at this grade level to guide us as to approximately what we can expect.
- Since in this case it is not a specific content that is to be learned, but a skill, we are already considering the examples by which this might be done, and the specific people to whom the text might be addressed.

Your example

3. *Reflect on Your Vision*

Develop a vision in your mind's eye of where the students will be at the end of the unit.

Our example:

- The students should write about something they have experienced that matters to them.
- They could write about a school or family event to share their experience, perhaps in a blog, or on social media, or as a wall journal.
- Readers could give likes and feedback, and in this way, students could learn to express themselves even more accurately.
- Teachers and peers could act as proofreaders, to whom students show the texts before publishing.

Your example:

4. *Specify Your Intentions*

Now specify your intentions. For the whole unit, put into words what is previously "visioned." This does not have to be so detailed, as we know, but for practice purposes we spell out the intentions here. Later, this step will also take the form of concrete *tasks*.

Our example:

At the end of the lesson, we want all students to be able to find a topic from their community that is worth describing and write a short text about it that contains the most important information about it. This should be accurate and easy to understand. They seek help from peers and the teacher if they have difficulties or if they are unsure what to write about. All students should read others' writing carefully and provide appreciative feedback. And, of course, they should be able to post their own text online themselves.

Your example:

What Next?

Of course, you don't have to strictly follow the suggested scheme, but it can be a help in case you have little experience in dealing with standards. Stick with it for a while and gain experience with it. Later, you will probably find your own style, for example, jumping from the vision directly to the meaningful tasks, but always keeping in mind the principles of backward planning.

Expand Your Repertoire of Challenging Goals

As we all know, school has long been dominated by the principle of transmission of knowledge. At least since the 1950s, with the taxonomy of Bloom and colleagues (1956), it has been obvious that the range of goals can and must be much broader than just acquiring knowledge and skills. We are not talking now about the excesses of formulating detailed learning objectives, but about the core of the project of Bloom and colleagues and other researchers as well, namely, to focus systematically on challenging objectives to foster students' abilities more comprehensively.

Taxonomies

Bloom distinguished six levels of increasing cognitive demand. They are hierarchical, that is, to get to the most demanding level, the previous ones should have been passed:

1. Knowledge 2. Comprehension 3. Application 4. Analysis 5. Synthesis 6. Evaluation

Decades later, Anderson and Krathwohl (2001) revised and differentiated this taxonomy and added the second dimension of knowledge forms (table 8.1).

However, this highly elaborated concept of learning goal taxonomy was not without its critics, especially since the distinction between cognitive processes can rarely be made in a discriminating way. Also, the distinction between the four forms of knowledge does not always seem compelling, for example, between factual and conceptual knowledge. Nevertheless, the model has had an inspiring effect on the formulation of goals because different perspectives can be synthesized in a reasonably coherent way.

Table 8.1.   The structure of the taxonomy of Anderson and Krathwohl (2001, p. 28).

		The Cognitive Process Dimension					
		1. Remember	2. Understand	3. Apply	4. Analyze	5. Evaluate	6. Create
The Knowledge Dimension	Factual Knowledge						
	Conceptual Knowledge						
	Procedural Knowledge						
	Metacognitive Knowledge						

Numerous other taxonomies have been proposed; for example, sometimes only a distinction is made between cognitively demanding and less demanding goals (high level, low level). The SOLO taxonomy, which builds on Piaget's theory of cognitive development, distinguishes five levels, from cognitive arbitrariness to highly abstract coherence (Biggs & Collis, 1982, pp. 24–25). Another taxonomy comes from Gagné et al. (1992); it is based on the different capacities of people (pp. 43–49):

Intellectual Skill:	*how to do* something, procedural knowledge
Cognitive Strategy:	the individual's own learning, remembering, and thinking behavior
Verbal Information:	knowing *that*, or declarative knowledge
Motor Skill:	making possible a motor performance
Attitude:	the choice of a course of personal action

It might be highly demanding, time consuming, and, in the end, rather unproductive if someone wants to use these taxonomies systematically for goal setting, unless they are an author of standards, curricula, or textbooks. Nonetheless, as the following tables show, taxonomies can give you ideas you might not otherwise have and remind you of goal areas you've lost sight of. So, expand your horizons of meaningful goals by drawing inspiration from taxonomies.

Broaden the Horizon of Learning Goals and Tasks

An example using the taxonomy of Anderson and Krathwohl

The example in table 8.2 uses the topic of carbon dioxide or CO_2 (at an introductory level) to show how taxonomies—in this case Anderson and Krathwohl's taxonomy—can stimulate teachers to broaden their range of tasks (as the materialization of goals). They also can use them to locate their blind spots, that is, target areas that they have not paid attention to so far. The following tasks go far beyond mere knowledge about CO_2, and each addresses other forms of knowledge and cognitive processes.

Another example that fans out the many facets of "understanding"

Understanding means having a deeper insight. But there is a difference in understanding a person or a mathematical operation or a novel. Wiggins and McTighe (2011) list six facets of understanding, each of which illuminates a different aspect of deeper insight:

- Explanation
- Interpretation
- Application
- Perspective
- Empathy
- Self-knowledge

If you are aware of these facets of deeper understanding, you will have a much larger repertoire when designing tasks. Students, for example, can understand a play in many ways, depending on which facet is emphasized. You can go through the six facets for yourself and apply them to the subject of the play, and you will discover the potential richness of including all facets. The task for "understanding a play" would be completely different in each individual case.

DESIGNING TASKS, USING EXISTING TASKS: THE PRACTICE OF USING RESOURCES

We know that good tasks are a manifestation of intentions. Conversely, we also know that some tasks are of poor quality—mundane, focused on unimportant things, too complicated, not focused on understanding, without apparent meaning, not challenging higher-order thinking. And again, this can be due to two things: the intentions were not clear, or the

Table 8.2. Tasks on carbon dioxide in the grid of Anderson and Krathwohl's taxonomy.

		The Cognitive Process Dimension					
		1. Remember	2. Understand	3. Apply	4. Analyze	5. Evaluate	6. Create
The Knowledge Dimension	Factual Knowledge	What term is also used to describe CO_2?	What in the following list is an element, a compound, or a mixture? Why? • distilled alcohol • air • tap water • steel • CO_2 • copper	Correct the errors in this sentence: "The mixture of coal K and oxygen X gives coal oxygen KX_2."	State which of the following gases make up more than 1% of the air: argon, hydrogen, oxygen, methane, chlorine gas, nitrogen, CO_2, water vapor, gasoline vapors.	How much did the amount of CO_2 in the atmosphere increase between 1900 and 2000? Compare the numerous online sources and choose the most plausible data.	Summarize at least four of the most typical properties of CO_2 in a single understandable, grammatically correct sentence.
	Conceptual Knowledge	What is the principle behind the fact that there are holes in bread?	Two balloons of exactly the same size are placed on the balance: one is filled with CO_2, the other with air. What will be observed? Justify.	A piece of wood is burned; at the end you can see some gray ash. Describe the process from a chemical point of view.	When a bottle of sparkling water is shaken, gaseous CO_2 is released. Describe which processes are involved, how they work, and how they differ.	There are fire extinguishers that emit CO_2 gas. What might be the advantages and disadvantages over those using water, powder, or foam?	You know several natural and artificial sources of CO_2. Think about how the ways of producing CO_2 could be classified in a meaningful way. You can also make several suggestions.
	Procedural Knowledge	Describe one method of detecting CO_2.	If you put a few drops of acid on a stone and it starts to foam, you know that it is limestone. How do you explain that?	Describe two ways you can make CO_2 using these substances: eggs, lemon, flour, sugar, water, baking powder, chocolate powder, yeast	List and justify the advantages and disadvantages of the "match method" for detecting CO_2.	Evaluate the following situation: a farmer places several open barrels of crushed fruit in a windowless cellar to make it sour. He must allow the fruit to ferment for two weeks.	Dry ice is frozen CO_2. When it thaws, it does not get wet, but evaporates. What would be useful applications of dry ice?
	Metacognitive Knowledge	What experiment led the seventeenth-century chemist van Helmont to claim that there must be an invisible substance, which he called "gas," and which would later prove to be CO_2?	Write a short letter or mail to a (fictional) friend. Explain to your friend the difficulties of recognizing and distinguishing gases and how to approach the problem.	It is difficult to discuss gases with nonexperts because gases are mostly invisible and odorless. What experiments would be particularly useful to illustrate the existence of gases (including van Helmont's experiment; see left)?	A newspaper article headlines: "Why Is CO_2 Bad?" Is it fair to ask this question? Investigate what might be meant by it, and correct it if necessary.	Some experiments on CO_2 need special substances and laboratory equipment, and some can be done at home with everyday substances. Compare the two approaches and discuss how and what you can learn about chemistry in each case.	Today, CO_2 is talked about in many ways, e.g., as a gas that creates a greenhouse effect. How could one proceed to explain to a layperson some useful and necessary, but also problematic and harmful, properties and applications of CO_2?

MAKING THE TASKS MEANINGFUL (GOALS THAT ADDRESS A WIDE RANGE OF CAPABILITIES)

Reminder:

Goals manifest themselves in tasks. When you design a task, you implicitly name the goal as well—but not the other way around. If you formulate goals, you do not yet have tasks.

1. *Your Topic*

Find any topic for this exercise: for example, based on the standards, based on a textbook, or something you want to teach or have already taught, or even a topic that you are not comfortable with and would like to find a new approach to. Don't choose the topic too narrowly—this way, you have greater latitude in developing goals and tasks.

Specific vs. open ended

The tasks or goals can be quite specific and thus easier to measure, like some tasks in the previous CO_2 example. Or, the tasks can be more open ended and "big," presenting genuine challenges for students to delve into, so-called big ideas. Both are possible and useful.

2. *Tasks or Test items That Use Anderson and Krathwohl's Taxonomy*

Previously, the example of CO_2 was used to show the variety possible when using all options suggested by Anderson and Krathwohl (2001).
Instead of anemic goals, look for lively tasks! Therefore, find as many tasks or test items as possible across all dimensions of Anderson and Krathwohl's taxonomy (2001).

3. *Big Ideas Aiming at Deep Understanding*

Big ideas often have a great motivational effect and encourage students to dig deeper. Furthermore, when it comes to really understanding something, the six facets of Wiggins and McTighe mentioned earlier are a great help. Whatever topic you choose: if you take one or more of these facets of understanding into account, the tasks take on a different character, and something else is learned particularly deeply.
Take the following steps:

1. Decide on a subject first, and within it a particular area, for example, short-story writing, American history, composition, solid geometry, or energy storage.
2. Within those areas, look for interesting, challenging problems to explore and deepen the topic. It's helpful to remember your own experiences: what problem engaged, intrigued, and inspired me to explore it further myself? What kind of task would interest *me*?
3. Next, design tasks that have the character of big ideas and are aimed at a deeper understanding of a topic.
4. Vary the tasks depending on which facet of understanding you are targeting.

To summarize: Subject → topic → big idea (a challenge) → facet of understanding → task

Further Reading

There is, besides textbooks, some further literature on how to design good tasks; it is recommended to go on reading (e.g., McTighe et al., 2020).

---

tasks are disconnected from the intentions. This is why the *strong tie between intentions and tasks* is so important.

When we teachers develop tasks, we do four things at once—and all four are important:

- We specify the intentions.
- We clarify the content (first and foremost for ourselves).
- We design student activities.
- We construct assessment tasks.

Therefore, developing tasks is an absolutely central activity of teachers—everything flows together here: intentions, content, activities, assessment.

Here Are Some Important Points When Designing Tasks on Your Own

1. Do not distinguish between tasks for activity and summative assessment

We know that a summative assessment examines what has been learned and practiced in class (using activities). Therefore, students must know what the subject of the assessment will be. They know that the tasks are going to be of the same nature as those tasks they have already dealt with. Thus, as discussed earlier, there is no reason to withhold the assessment tasks from the students. Your only "secret" will be which of the tasks you will choose for the summative assessment.

2. *For the lesson, use your preliminary work done in the planning of the unit*

The intentions have already been outlined in a set of tasks while planning the unit. These tasks are usually very authentic because the teacher has invested a lot of thought work.

3. *Follow some practical rules and hints for good tasks*

The box further down gives some commonly known rules for task construction, on the one hand the well-known SMART concept, and on the other hand a list of mistakes to avoid. And have a look again at the previous boxes.

Hints and Pitfalls When Using Existing Task Collections

1. *Do not underestimate the effort required to understand third-party tasks*

Existing collections of tasks in textbooks and on the internet, worksheets, educational software, and so on are certainly useful for keeping students engaged. What at first seems like a relief sometimes turns out to be more difficult than expected. The teacher does not yet know the tasks, has to study them first and solve them if necessary.

2. *The tasks do not always fit the lesson exactly*

Some tasks are too easy, too difficult, or they use different linguistic expressions, have different premises and unfamiliar presentation, and so on. The effort to explain this to the students or to rewrite the tasks might be too much.

3. *Do not fall for appealing graphic design*

Many tasks are attractively constructed and presented, but beware: it can also be just a sham if the tasks are insubstantial or if they are banal and repetitive.

4. There are tasks without learning effect

Some tasks are simply useless—you learn nothing, or the wrong thing. In many cases they are constructed only to keep the students busy and still (e.g., coloring).

5. Do a simple quality test on tasks you take over from somewhere else

The quality of a task is expressed in three aspects:

- In terms of content: Does the task *contain the necessary information* and no factual errors?
- In terms of intent: Does the task *really help to learn what is intended*?
- In terms of form: Is the task *well constructed*—understandable, solvable, motivating?

How to proceed with the quality test is described in a box on the next pages.

Nevertheless, It's a Sign of Professionalism to Draw on Existing Ideas

Teachers who think they have to invent everything themselves are wasting their time, which they then lack for more important things. There are so many ready-made and well-considered tasks out there, so many materials and lesson plans. It would be absurd not to use these resources.

Teachers have to acquire *practices of finding and using other people's resources* efficiently and effectively. Therefore, using existing designs and materials wisely and effectively must be rated highly. Those who honor the excellent work of others and use and optimize it as the basis of their own teaching deserve credit. This is not accompanied by a loss of autonomy; the teacher continues to make decisions and is relieved of the time-consuming and exhausting task of reinvention.

One Last Point: No Minimalism

Using what is available should not amount to minimalism. The time and energy gained should not only be used for one's own convenience but should be invested in all the really important tasks for which the teacher is an expert: engaging with students; recognizing difficulties and potential; explaining, supporting, and clarifying; facilitating productive experiences; guiding social and cognitive learning; encouraging and radiating confidence; mediating in conflicts—and much more.

Further Information and Resources

BE SMART

The SMART checklist for management goals (Doran, 1981) has been widely applied worldwide because it is useful and immediately plausible. It has also been adapted for educational purposes. It works very well not only for goals but also for tasks. Construct or adapt tasks or check their quality according to the following formal aspects:

- **S = Specific (also: simple, sensible, significant)**—The task must be formulated precisely and understandable for everyone
- **M = Measurable (also: meaningful, motivating)**—"Measurable" for simpler tasks, "meaningful" and "motivating" for more complex tasks
- **A = Achievable (also: agreed, attainable)**—Key criterion; possibly differentiate depending on prior knowledge of the students
- **R = Relevant (also: reasonable, realistic, resourced)**—Relevant in the sense of: beneficial to learning, helpful to achieve the goal
- **T = Time bound (also: time based, time limited, timely)**—Not as a strict deadline, but as a realistic estimate of the required time

AVOID THESE MISTAKES WHEN DESIGNING TASKS

Mistake 1: Your tasks are too demanding

Overly complex tasks can overwhelm many students and lead to frustration. They have a greater sense of achievement, more enjoyment, and faster progress if they work on more tasks that are solvable and in the "learning zone" or the "zone of proximal development."

How to do better: Try to offer more but not too complex tasks. Exception: if you work with big ideas and carefully guide students in solving more complex problems, see mistake 2.

Mistake 2: You offer too little help with challenging tasks

Of course, challenging tasks are important, but support must be provided (factual, technical, emotional, strategic) for learning and enjoyment to occur.

How to do better: Include hints in the tasks if possible. Offer help if needed.

Mistake 3: You insist on the one solution

Constant testing has instilled in students that mistakes are a bad thing, and yet in all areas of life, such as living together, thinking, sports, and science, one learns heavily from mistakes.

How to do better: Construct tasks at times so that there are multiple solutions or that seemingly wrong solutions can still lead to constructive discussions.

Mistake 4: You want everyone to do everything

Not all students need to solve all or the same tasks. Remain flexible to keep all students in the "learning zone": assign different or more or fewer tasks, give more time, solve tasks only partially. This allows all to progress where they currently are.

How to do better: Provide similar tasks with different levels of difficulty so that you can differentiate in class.

Mistake 5: You take over tasks from others without understanding them yourself

As emphasized earlier, it is disastrous when students *and* teachers have difficulty with a task.

How to do better: Only use tasks that you yourself really understand and consider suitable.

Mistake 6: You assign tasks for homework that cannot be solved with certainty

Few things undermine learning as much as homework that is too difficult. Apart from cheating, it often introduces wrong things that you have to fix and causes anger among students and at home.

How to do better: Always construct assignments for homework that can be sure to be solved without error, such as by including instructions or solutions, or choose open-ended assignments, for example: "Tomorrow, bring the packaging of six foods that list the ingredients. Divide them into those that contain sugar and those that do not."

CONCLUSION

Where do we stand in terms of goals and expected results in a unit? Let's summarize in six steps how we move from standards to specific intentions (i.e., desired outcomes) and tasks aligned to those intentions.

1. Standards

We have considered the standards or other guidelines.

2. Own Ideas

We have introduced our own significant ideas.

3. Intentions/Desired Results

We decide what we want to achieve with the students; the intentions (i.e., the desired results) have become clear.

4. Tasks

The desired results are expressed in the form of tasks (activities, assessment, and from it the students can recognize the success criteria). The guiding question is: *What does the exam look like that proves students have really learned what I expect?*

5. Quality

We draw on our knowledge of good and not-so-good tasks when constructing or searching for tasks, and use a wide range of requirement levels.

6. Content

On the basis of the tasks, we make sure that the content is completely clear for ourselves.

Now we know what students should and can achieve in a unit—not as abstract statements, but in the form of specific tasks and challenges. This is the firm foundation on which each lesson will be built. Next, we will look at how the transition from unit to lesson occurs.

ACTIVITIES AND SUGGESTIONS

FINDING AND CHECKING THIRD-PARTY TASKS AND MATERIALS; FILING YOUR WORK

The basic approach is simple: Look around, do a quality check, don't fall for pleasingly designed tasks, don't be too comfortable.

Here is a *suggestion* of the procedure to create a collection of tasks and materials of good quality.

Step 1: Find Tasks and Materials

Develop the "utilitarian gaze"

Develop or keep the utilitarian gaze, which is not atypical for teachers: you constantly look around to see if you can find something that would be stimulating, meaningful, and suitable for teaching, or even more—reality is viewed through the lens of being useful for teaching. This can be criticized, but in this context, it is a useful thing.

Routinely scan the most promising sources

Such sources might include textbooks, courses on teaching and learning, professional journals, online resources, tips from colleagues, your own lesson plans and materials, and so forth. Ask your colleagues where they get their materials.

Do you see at first glance that something is useless? Ignore it

You should be able to judge with a quick glance whether the tasks and materials would even be suitable for you or your class. If you immediately see that the material is unsuitable, then don't waste any more time on it.

Your first reactions to these proposals:

- Do I work this way?
- Do I proceed more intuitively or more systematically?
- Do I tend to accumulate material, or on the contrary, am I constantly missing something?

Step 2: Make a Quality Check (If Necessary)

In this step, try out the quality check with a topic for which you have already selected or designed tasks, or analyze existing tasks, for example, from a textbook or worksheet. After each of the following paragraphs, you will be asked to do a short quality check on the respective tasks. Just write down a few keywords.

Content: Does each task contain the necessary information and no factual errors?

Often, but especially in history, social studies, and science, tasks are embedded in a context that is different from your own unit. If you cannot correct it in a simple way, the task is no good, unless the basic idea of the task can be reasonably adopted and adapted.

- Check that the content of your tasks is informative and correct

Intent: Does the task really help to learn what is intended?

The task must fit into the goals of your own unit. If it practices something you are not aiming for at all, it is useless.

- Check what the goals of the task actually are

Form: Are the tasks well constructed—understandable, solvable, motivating?

See preceding box.

- Check whether the tasks are technically well constructed

Step 3: File Your Tasks, Unit Plans, and Lesson Plans Purposefully

Invest in building a logical filing system

You need a filing system that suits you and that you enjoy using. Don't leave it to chance, or you'll have tons of materials piling up on your shelves, hard drives and clouds that you can't even use.

Your system doesn't have to be perfect, just in such a way that you can file things in an orderly manner and also find them again. You don't create such a filing system from one day to the next. So take your time, stay pragmatic, and remember that you will probably work with it for years.

Sketch out here your initial ideas of how you envision such a system. If you have already started with it:

- How does it work?

- What should you change?

Step 4: Exchange Ideas

Exchange ideas with colleagues

You don't have to reinvent the wheel—every teacher has experience with sifting, using, and filing materials. Ask around and test what works for you.

- Jot down some colleagues, peers, friends, forums, chats, and so on where you can share:

9

∞

From Unit to Lesson

Two Goals per Lesson, and Assessment

Several times now, the transparent opening of the lesson has been mentioned. Basically, the idea is clear: the students will be informed what today's lesson is about and will not be left in the dark. In other words, they should and want to be briefly and concisely updated on the content, intentions, and flow of the lesson. This is actually a matter of course that is generally common among adults, and this is how it should be handled with students as well (see box "The Transparent Opening").

Teachers who have done unit planning, including providing the relevant tasks, have a clear picture of their intentions. But now one's intentions have to be portioned out, so to speak, and adapted to the current conditions. Moreover, unlike units, lessons are comparatively short. Thus, the goals are usually manageable and not overly complex, and thus they are easier to transmit. How we find and communicate such lesson goals is what we are talking about here.

THE BASIS IS THE GOALS, SET IN THE UNIT—
NOW THE STUDENTS COME INTO PLAY

It's true to say that the decisions made so far about the goals and desired results have been pretty abstract, because the real students haven't even entered the picture yet. But once we set the cornerstones of the particular lesson, the moment has come when the rubber meets the road.

The one important resource is, of course, the *planning of the unit*. In it, the important things for a series of several lessons are already decided.

Within this framework is to be determined what needs to be accomplished and done in a single lesson. To make a comparison: if the unit is a novel, then the lesson is a short story (with a few characters, a single plot, one place, at a specific time).

The second important resource is *knowledge about the students* who are to learn and understand something. Teaching, after all, only makes sense if it is adapted to the addressees. So, the teacher considers what the students have already learned or not learned, what they need and at what level, how much will be possible in a lesson for these students, what circumstances might facilitate or impede learning, what differences there are among individual students, and so forth. Without this adaptation of teaching to students, instruction makes little sense. It sounds like a lot of effort, but it's not if you know your students a little.

During unit planning, the teacher has sufficiently addressed the intentions, the content, and the tasks. Now the teacher must shift perspective and look and think from the students' point of view, empathize with them, and decide with understanding what makes the most sense for the lesson to resonate with the students.

To accomplish this, we stick to the "two goals and assessment" heuristic. That's not simplistic, it's essentializing. A lesson is short, and it needs a focus on a few things, but then they can really be learned.

1. One Subject-Based Goal: Choose a Topic with a Learning Focus

Why Just One Goal?

Throw me a tennis ball and I'll catch it. Throw me three balls, and I catch none.

Sometimes teachers—especially the less experienced ones—want to pack too much into a lesson. This creates stress for everyone, particularly toward the end of the lesson when the work is not finished, things are not really understood, and there is no time left for summing up.

That's why it makes sense to limit yourself to *one* subject-related goal—a goal that can be reliably understood in a lesson by all who are engaged in the work. Achieving the goal should take at most two-thirds of the lesson, so that there is still time for "overlearning" and summing up, or for unforeseen things.

Of course, it would be possible to set many more sub-objectives, which would only complicate everything. The sub-objectives are obvious from the tasks and do not need to be formulated, as has been discussed several times.

The topic and learning focus can be expressed in a quasi-abstract way, but it is only with the *intentions* (expressed in tasks) that it becomes clear what students can and should learn. This is illustrated in table 9.1.

The Transparent Opening

The opening informs students about what is to follow. The transparent opening is an expression of a partner-like relationship between the teacher and the learners. By providing transparent and clear information about what is to follow, the students are taken seriously as people with whom a goal is to be achieved. The transparent opening is far from any staging. It does not use tricks, gimmicks to motivate, or manipulation, and it does not "motivate" in order to attract students to the lesson and the subject matter. It simply says what it is all about.

The unspoken message underlying this sort of opening is sober and honest. It might be something like, "We are gathered here so that you can learn something about a particular topic. I will try to explain to you why it is important and perhaps useful, and I will make an effort so that you will not have come to school for nothing, and that you will know and be able to do more afterward than you did before. And I'll do my part so that we can work in a cheerful and productive learning atmosphere."

Addressing students in this way treats them as partners in the common enterprise of learning and allows them to participate in what is happening. To do so, you as a teacher have three decisions to make in advance of each particular lesson:

1. *One subject-based goal*: Choose a topic (based on the unit planning) with a learning focus for that lesson and decide what you want to accomplish with it.
2. *One cross-curricular goal*: Think about your students and decide what they should learn as a matter of priority, in addition to the subject matter aspect.
3. *Assessment*: Set tasks or choose other forms of assessment, as well as comprehensible criteria, so that you yourself and all students can always see where they stand, what progress they are making, and what still needs to be learned.

2. One Cross-Curricular Goal: What Is Important for Learners Now

Teachers could simply settle for thematic goals. But in doing so, they would miss a unique pedagogical opportunity and also neglect their educational mission. Young people have things to learn outside the subject standards, and a teacher who is sensitive to these learning needs can and should address them.

Only the teacher can determine what is urgent right now and right here, for example, in terms of learning strategies, self-organization, social skills, and, at times, personal issues and practical matters of everyday school life. Since many standards, such as the Common Core State Standards in the United States, are primarily subject oriented, the cross-curricular goals are sometimes lost from view. Nevertheless, there seems to be a general consensus that these capacities are very important, for example, in the social area ("supporting each other in teams") or methodological skills ("being able to inform yourself about an issue").

Table 9.1. The subject-based goal: from topic/learning focus to intention/task to assessment, with three examples.

Topic (given by the unit)	Learning Focus (to be defined for this very lesson)	→	Intention Expressed in a Task (if you don't find a meaningful intention, the learning focus doesn't make sense either)	→	Assessment (using only tasks that students are familiar with)
Examples:					
Topic: Different ways of life	*Learning focus:* Use interviews to document them	→	Have direct conversations with people of, for example, different cultural characteristics, ages, community types, religious lifestyles, and report whether and how they have expanded your ideas about less familiar ways of living.	→	Use these and similar tasks for formative and summative assessment
Topic: Small commercial enterprises (e.g., bakery, carpentry)	*Learning focus:* Research on how they work	→	Ask a responsible person in this small enterprise what is the role and importance of some factors for success, for example, labor (skills, manners), material, machinery, information, marketing, good relationships, innovation.	→	Use these and similar tasks for formative and summative assessment
Topic: Musical notation	*Learning focus:* Note music yourself	→	Pass on your own musical idea (fifteen to thirty seconds) to others as accurately as possible, but only in writing.	→	Use these and similar tasks for formative and summative assessment

Created by the author

Even if it is not always explicitly required of teachers who teach a subject, no one disputes that the school also has to teach generic skills. Given the specific lesson, the teacher now has to develop a clear intention: What is now relevant or necessary for most students or the whole class? (We are not talking about individualized goals at this point; those are the subject of individualized learning support.)

It is your personal decision what you want to make a cross-curricular goal—and if at all. But it would be unwise and unprofessional to pass up this opportunity. You should practice setting *one* meaningful generic goal at a time and open it up for discussion. And refer to this goal at the end of the lesson when summing up. This is the only way you can show the students that you really care.

Here are just a few examples from different areas:

- In group work, make sure all group members are on the same page.
- When working with partners, speak only in whispers so that others are not disturbed.
- Those who sit at the computer or use smartphones only work on the tasks and do not allow themselves to be distracted.
- We manage time well and stop on time (this also applies to me as a teacher).
- We present results on the flip chart so clearly that they are understandable at first glance.
- If you get stuck while working on a task, I expect you to describe as precisely as possible where the problem is so that others can provide you with focused support.

To make it clear once again: You decide on cross-curricular or generic intentions situationally, that is, when the situation requires it or when the opportunity presents itself to work on it. It should become a matter of course that you always explicitly formulate a non-subject-specific intention as well. Again: just one cross-curricular goal, that's enough. Make sure progress is made in that one goal.

And don't forget: at the end of the lesson, refer again to the goals, especially to this cross-curricular goal, and ask the students to what extent they have achieved it.

3. The Assessment: How We Find Out Where We Stand

Wiggins and McTighe (2011) recommend to "think like an assessor" when determining and reviewing expected outcomes. For many people, this idea has a negative connotation and is reminiscent of unpleasant experiences with testing. However, this is not meant to be the case. After all, it is mostly about obtaining evidence and about progress toward the expected results. As table 9.2 shows, only a small part of the assessment is experienced as emotionally stressful—high-stakes testing in the fourth column.

What is expected as a result must always be transparent, as we know. A teacher will inform students about it as a matter of course. And by knowing the tasks, the students also know the goals. It is, after all, one of the pillars of backward planning that teachers and students agree from the outset where they will stand together at the end.

As a teacher, you have to know where you and your students stand *now*; otherwise, teaching is a blind flight. Teachers can find out primarily through appreciative formative and summative assessment; this is an ongoing task and an important source of information. Tests are never the

Table 9.2. Overview of the different forms and functions of assessment (see also Dolin et al., 2017, p. 68).

	Formative Assessment of Process and Progress		Summative Assessment of Performance	
What to Do	Observe and listen; analyze students' products, essays, etc.; have conversations	Informally question students in writing	Formally test students; systematically assess student products, under the fairest possible conditions	
What For	To understand and support students	To know where the class stands; evaluate own teaching	Low-stakes tests to assess performance, understanding, behavior	High-stakes grading for career decisions and accountability
When	Always	Now and then as needed	Once per unit or more	Less than once per unit
For Whom	For the students	For the teacher	For teacher and students	For schools and districts
Remarks	It happens almost constantly and informally with responsive teachers. The teacher wants to know how learning is progressing for individual students; this formative diagnosis can take many different forms and is one of the core practices of teachers.	Sometimes the teacher wants to know if the teaching approach is triggering the desired effects; this is about providing feedback to the teacher in order to continue or readjust instruction as effectively as possible. Classroom assessment techniques (CATs) can be used (see box in chapter 10).	The teacher will need to conduct a summative assessment of students from time to time to ascertain learning levels as accurately as possible. It is informative for both students and teachers to take stock and compare actual performance with expected results.	High-stakes tests are the basis for many decisions, such as whether students receive a diploma or advance to the next grade level, how successful the teacher is judged to be, or how a school performs overall.

best option for this. Results of tests, even short and informal ones, are always delayed and often give only a vague overall impression. It is usually too late to respond and remediate.

While high-stakes tests may seem necessary, they are limited, isolated events and should not overshadow everyday school life. The actual practices of checking expected results now go in several directions, as table 9.2 shows. Yes, such tables are often overlooked because they seem to be hard to read and interpret. In this case, resist the temptation not to look at it closely; read it carefully column by column and row by row. It concisely summarizes many essential insights on learning in class and assessment.

ACTIVITIES AND SUGGESTIONS

THREE SIMPLE DECISIONS TO CLARIFY THE EXPECTED RESULTS OF A LESSON

Preliminary remark: This activity makes sense especially if you are going to teach yourself in the near future. If this is not the case, you should consequently omit the second point (cross-curricular goal).

The three decisions you need to make for a specific lesson have now been described. These three items are basically quite simple. You might say these decisions form the backbone of the lesson. Practice these three decisions; once you have made them consciously and clearly, everything else will be easier. At the beginning of each lesson, disclose these decisions (see box "The Transparent Opening").

1. *One subject-based goal*

   Choose a topic (based on the unit planning) with a learning focus for that lesson and decide what you want to accomplish with it.

2. *One cross-curricular goal*

   Think about your students and decide what they should learn as a matter of priority, in addition to the subject matter aspect.

3. *Assessment*

   Set tasks or choose other forms of assessment, as well as comprehensible criteria, so that you yourself and all students can always see where they stand, what progress they are making, and what still needs to be learned.

Note how you make these decisions most effectively. This whole complex of deciding what the teacher actually wants in a lesson is quite challenging for less experienced teachers, precisely because the result (three clear messages) must be simple.

Therefore, the recommendations

- Make your own little checklist for these three decisions.
- Give yourself tips.
- Warn yourself about pitfalls.
- Show yourself how to formulate your intentions and expectations simply and really well.

And don't forget: if you increasingly succeed in making decisions pragmatically and professionally, record that, too. It does you good to become aware of your successes.

FURTHER INFORMATION AND RESOURCES

FAR-REACHING AND WORRISOME EFFECTS OF ASSESSMENT CONCEPTS ON TEACHERS AND STUDENTS

It is easy to say that formative and summative assessment should be separated, but in practice difficulties arise nonetheless. This problem has been addressed in particular by Black (2015) and Dolin and colleagues (2017). Dolin and colleagues (2017) analyzed eight different countries' practices of formative assessment and the difficulties in implementing them, often due to domination of summative assessment. As for linking formative and summative use of assessment, these variations seem relevant, as they state:

> Recognition of the need to share goals and assessment criteria with students, which may require teachers to reformulate the goals and criteria so that they can be understood by students, is a procedure that is not common practice in all countries.
>   Clarity about the formative or summative status of any assessment event: In some countries it is the expectation of the students, and their parents, to be told when the student's product is to be used for summative assessment. This information affects the way students respond to a task; if a more formative purpose is in-

tended, errors are seen as something that can help learning, while if the task is seen as for summative assessment, errors are seen as indicating that a learning goal has not been met. To put this another way, students may perform in one way if they understand that their products will be used (and judged) in order to improve their learning but may perform in a quite different way if they know the product will be judged for summative purposes. . . . If students know that the report has a formative purpose, they will be more experimental, more open and less tactical and will strive less for perfection, for flawless work.

The balance between assessment for accountability purposes and assessment for learning or the dominance of a testing regime on everyday practice: National tests and the stakes of the examinations have a strong influence on teachers' teaching and students' behaviour. . . . No matter how much teachers emphasize the formative purpose of an assessment, the summative element does not disappear. *Students do seldom believe that any assessment only has a formative purpose, given today's reality in contemporary educational systems.* (pp. 70–71, emphasis mine)

10

∞

More on Assessment

On the following pages, some aspects of assessment are now dealt with in greater detail. In addition, an excursus dedicated to the written exams follows at the end.

INFORMAL ASSESSMENT AT CLASS LEVEL
HELPS YOU IMPROVE AS A TEACHER

Informal assessment is an excellent way to make your own instruction fairer and better. Sure, one may ask whether an assessment at class level is needed at all, when learning is always individual. The answer is yes, it is needed as long as teaching is organized in a class or learning group. The teacher does not always have the necessary information about the overall level of learning at hand. Where does the class stand? Who could not follow? Where are the difficulties? Who has understood thoroughly, who not yet? Why is there resistance to learning? How do I need to readjust?

Obtain Reliable Evidence, but as Informal as Possible

It can be seen as a practice of its own, with which the teacher obtains such information quickly and without much fuss. After all, experienced teachers know that students are not very forthcoming when it comes to revealing learning needs, especially when it involves extra work. Therefore, general questions about understanding are usually unproductive. Those who ask, "Did you understand that?" or "Who else has a question?"

cannot count on learners coming forward with their real learning problems. At best, learners notice that they are not keeping up, but they are usually not yet able or willing to immediately formulate a precise question. They probably don't even know what exactly they didn't understand. Other strategies are needed to learn about students' learning levels.

In the following box "Techniques for Obtaining Feedback," a number of simple procedures are described to get a quick overview (classroom assessment techniques, CATs for short). Many teachers have these and similar techniques at their disposal in order to use them in the right way at the right time.

FURTHER INFORMATION AND RESOURCES

TECHNIQUES FOR OBTAINING FEEDBACK: CLASSROOM ASSESSMENT TECHNIQUES (CATS)

For decades, the body of suggestions for simple ways to elicit students' knowledge, interests, difficulties, suggestions, and opinions has been growing. Many of the ideas in Angelo and Cross's (1993) extensive summary have been expanded and varied over the years. While much of the suggestions in the following compilation derive from Angelo and Cross's classroom assessment techniques (CATs), they are found in many sources in varying forms; for some, the original source can no longer be determined, or they are simply part of the profession's commonly known body of techniques. If you browse the resources and blogs available online now and then, you'll keep coming across new variations.

Formative evaluation and anonymity

For all of the following techniques, student feedback is usually anonymous unless there would be an important reason for the teacher to know the names. The point, after all, is not to evaluate individual students, but to get an overall picture of how successful learning has been and where there are deficiencies. It must be made clear to all students that these are formative evaluations and feedback that will not be used for performance evaluation.

Always communicate the time frame and have the material ready

In many cases, these techniques are used at the end of an activity or lesson. To avoid stress, a reasonable amount of time should be allotted, and students should know how much time they have. The materials (notes, questionnaires, etc.) should always be at hand.

Use digital tools as well

Digital tools and media can also be used for many of the following suggestions if they are already established in the classroom: chat groups, feedback
apps, mails, forums, blogs, and so forth.

Vary!

All suggestions can be varied depending on the subject, level, and circumstances, so that they are as informative as possible for the teacher and
answer the question at hand as well as possible.

A Dozen Suggestions

*1. What prior knowledge do students bring along? Technique: "Elicit
   prior knowledge and attitudes"*

What it is about:
For effective teaching, the teacher needs to know what students already
know and can do. Sometimes the teacher may already be aware of it. But
sometimes a short survey is the most effective way to find out. The teacher
will learn where to start and at what level the majority of the students are,
and where there are problems or potential. And it becomes transparent
how far apart the learning levels of the students are.

What to pay attention to:
- Do the survey the day before; if the survey is conducted right at the
  beginning of the lesson, it is difficult or even impossible to adapt the
  lesson to the previous knowledge.
- Explain the purpose of the survey.
- What exactly should be asked? Prior knowledge of the lesson?
  Attitudes? Interest?
- Question type: yes/no questions, scale from 1 to 5, and so forth, or
  open-ended questions.

*2. Where do the students stand after this learning phase? Technique:
   "Postcard"*

What it is about:
This technique is simple and self-evident. Instead of asking the class and
expecting verbal feedback, the teacher asks students to provide brief
written feedback about their learning, usually near the end of a lesson.
The length is limited, such as half a sheet of paper, or just a postcard.
The teacher asks short and simple questions, for example, "What do you

remember most about this lesson?" or "What do you continue to struggle with?" or "Of what you learned, what is most important?" Students write down their answers and hand them in.

What to pay attention to:
- Communicate whether a particular form is desired (e.g., complete sentences, keywords).
- Prepare questions ahead of time, and maybe even write them down for all to see.
- Announce when the notes will be commented on.

3. Was the teaching understandable and comprehensible?
Technique: "Muddiest point"

What it is about:
This technique is simple and efficient. The teacher learns where problems exist in a very short time. Angelo and Cross call the technique "muddiest point," meaning something that was unclear or incomprehensible. Students briefly respond in writing to the question, "What was the muddiest point in this lesson [this input, this text, this discussion, etc.]?"

What to pay attention to:
- Decide on what feedback is desired.
- Schedule when the teacher will give feedback.

4. How well can students argue? Technique: "Pros and cons"

What it is about:
Students outline a list of pros and cons on an issue that might require an opinion or decision. This CAT provides the teacher with information about students' ability to consider different points of view.

What to pay attention to:
- The teacher presents a situation in which a position must be taken—a dilemma or a problem that is relevant in the context of the subject matter, for example, "Transporting goods by air is sometimes controversial. What are the reasons for it, and what are the reasons against it?"
- The teacher can also present a pointed position for discussion, for which arguments for and against are to be noted.
- If necessary, specify the minimum number of arguments and a structure (e.g., two columns on a sheet).

5. *Do students know what matters? Technique: "Student-generated test questions"*

What it is about:
The benefits of this activity are immense. It allows the teacher to learn what the students consider to be the most important concepts in the unit, and to receive, virtually as a by-product, formulated tasks and test items about them, at least in a raw version.

What to pay attention to:
- Step 1. Have the students create questions and have them tested.
  - Students are given ample time to write their own test questions. The questions should allow to show the essence of the learning unit.
  - The assignment must be clear: it is about this learning unit and about the essential competencies (e.g., not just questions that recall factual knowledge).
  - In the question format, students should be free.
  - Students test each other's questions and assess them for comprehensibility, difficulty, and relevance.
- Step 2. Discuss congruence of questions with the core intentions of the unit.
  - A class discussion is recommended on what the key learning expectations of the unit were.
  - Students should discuss the extent to which the questions really make visible whether someone understood the core of the learning unit.
  - The teacher raises the prospect that some of the questions will be used for formative or summative evaluation.

6. *Did the students really understand the issue? Technique: "Mail to laypeople"*

What it is about:
Have students explain a fact they have just worked on in their own words in a short letter, mail, blog post, or the like, aimed at people with little prior knowledge. This technique is particularly useful when a deeper understanding of a context or issue is needed.

What to pay attention to:
- The teacher describes to the students exactly what issue they should present in a simple way.

- The text is framed in an appropriate way, for example: Addressee: "Explain to your grandmother / your friend / your WhatsApp group"; Issue: "How X works / What you have learned about X / What you now understand about X."
- Students should use simple language and only those technical terms that they are sure the addressees are familiar with.
- Students are given a realistic time frame.
- The teacher is going to read the texts to see what the students have understood and will inform the students to what extent the texts will affect the future lessons.
- If appropriate, the teacher can use a few of the students' examples for subsequent lessons.

7. Are the goals appropriate and achievable for the students? Technique: "Mutual alignment of intentions or goals"

What it is about:
The point here is for learners and teachers to agree on realistic goals. It is ideal if both are pulling together. The teacher announces the goals, but are they the students' goals? The goals of teacher and students may be too far apart, for example, students want repetitive practice, the teacher wants deeper mathematical understanding. Thus, the interest of the learners decreases and with it the learning progress. With a short survey, the teacher may get more authentic answers than in a class discussion, and the students learn to think about their goals. This is the basis for adjusting the goals together.

This technique is challenging, but if you can find common goals that teachers and students fully accept, your class will have taken a very big step toward becoming a productive learning community.

What to pay attention to:
- The teacher first clarifies for themselves again the intentions and considers to what extent the intentions can be adapted depending on the reaction of the students (if the goals are not adaptable, this CAT makes no sense).
- The teacher informs the class in a relatively general way about the topic of the unit or lesson and asks the students what they would like to achieve on this topic. Now, there are two possibilities:
  - Option 1: Simply, a class discussion takes place on this question if the learners have learned to talk openly and to the point about such matters and the teacher is willing to listen to their objections and arguments.

- Option 2: Students write down on a piece of paper two to three things that they think they would like to accomplish or can accomplish in this unit (at least one content goal and one cross-curricular goal each). Then have students rank them in order of importance (numbers 1, 2, 3, etc.). To quickly keep track, colored slips of paper can also be used, with each color having a meaning (e.g., importance). Then all slips of paper are laid out and the class gets an overview. Divergent and concordant goals are identified. Together, the need for action is determined (e.g., "This clearly seems too difficult," "Many are more interested in . . . ," "Some would first like to consolidate what they have learned so far before we continue," "I, as the teacher, will be especially available for those who find the goals too challenging").

8. How do students proceed while working? Technique: "Process analysis"

What it is about:

This suggestion takes a little more time. You don't need a separate time slot for this activity; it goes like this: in parallel to the usual work on a task, students write down *how* they solve the task.

With this analysis, the teacher learns what thinking processes and strategies the students use, and at the same time the students learn to think about their own strategies and thinking (metacognition). It is not about solving a task "correctly," but about becoming aware of the steps. An analysis can be good and enlightening, even if the task is solved incorrectly.

What to pay attention to:
- It is important that students not only solve the (interesting and solvable) task, but more importantly write down what steps and missteps they chose.
- Students should not be praised for finding the correct solution, but for accurately visualizing the process.
- Do not impose rigid formal requirements; instead, allow everyday language.
- Do not judge the process or the solution too quickly; sometimes strange, unexpected, and original ways also lead to the goal.

The analysis of the process can vary:
- Students write down all the steps; the teacher, in turn, analyzes the process and reports back or present their findings for discussion.

- Students use their notes to report what they thought about and how they proceeded.
- The class compares and discusses the different approaches.

9. *Where is the shoe pinching? Technique: "Mailbox"*

What it is about:
A mailbox by the classroom door allows students to anonymously post notes, suggestions, and criticisms about class or subject matter.

What to pay attention to:
- The mailbox is placed so that students can post their feedback unobserved.
- If necessary, formulate rules about the tone of the feedback (no insults, no sweeping judgments, etc.).

The teacher empties the mailbox periodically and informs the class about the feedback and how the teacher deals with it.

10. *How do students work together? Technique: "Evaluation of group work"*

What it is about:
Group work is sometimes opaque—it remains unclear what each has contributed and learned. A simple evaluation can help here and also raise awareness of group collaboration in the medium term. The teacher will know which group the student was in, but otherwise the feedback can remain anonymous.

What to pay attention to:
- Prepare a short questionnaire to be filled out by all students who have participated in group work, something like the example shown in the box below.
- The teacher reviews the questionnaires and presents the observations for discussion at the next opportunity; or, the groups exchange ideas after completing the questionnaires and make suggestions for more efficient work.

11. *How do students experience a summative assessment?*
Technique: "Students give feedback after summative tests"

What it is about:
This suggestion is easy to implement, very effective, and much appreciated by students. After all, during tests, most students are under stress and

Evaluation of Group Work: Example of a Questionnaire

Your group
   Group No.
   Number of members
Overall, how effective was the way you worked together?
   ☐ Not effective at all
   ☐ Somewhat ineffective
   ☐ Somewhat effective
   ☐ Very effective
How many group members actively participated most of the time?
   Number:
How many of you were fully prepared for the group work most of the time?
   Number:
Give an example of something you learned from the group that you probably would not have learned on your own.

Give an example of something the other group members learned from you that they probably would not have learned otherwise.

What could the group do to improve collaboration and performance?

---

pressure to perform, and they care about fair assessment. Therefore, the teacher gives students time and opportunity at the end of the test to provide meta-level feedback on summative assessments (tests, classwork, etc.). Informal feedback at the end of the test can provide the teacher with useful background information, and students have an opportunity to explain themselves and their performance.

What to pay attention to:
   • Allow some time at the end of each exam for students to respond in writing.
   • The teacher may leave it open to what is commented on and how, or ask questions like these:
      ○ "How well were you able to demonstrate your skills in this test?"

- ○ "If you are not satisfied with your performance, what could you change?"
- ○ "Is there anything that made it difficult for you to perform at your best today?"
- ○ "What grade do you think is appropriate for your performance?"
- ○ "If you don't think the test was fair, what is the reason?"

12. *How can we improve working, climate, and learning? Technique: "Feedback group"*

What it is about:
The teacher meets with a small group of students on a regular basis to share ideas about instruction, progress, opportunities for improvement, climate, and so forth.

What to pay attention to:
- Once implemented, the feedback group contributes greatly to good teaching, well-being, and learning.
- This form of feedback is comparatively time consuming.
- Participation in such a group must be voluntary for the students.
- And, of course, the teacher must be able to keep an open mind and listen without defending or justifying themselves.

Tests Stress and Steal Time

Caution seems to be warranted with *formal achievement tests,* even if they are only formative (low-stakes tests). Tests usually increase attention and tension because most students do not like to take tests. It then becomes less about learning and more about delivering a well-judged performance. Achievement tests provoke precisely this mode of performance, even when they are purely formative. For students, the focus is less on "What can I do (yet)?" and more on "Was I good? How many points did I score?" (cf. box "Far-Reaching and Worrisome Effects of Assessment Concepts on Teachers and Students" at the end of the preceding chapter). CATs, on the other hand, avoid whenever possible this testing mode of right or wrong; rather, they focus on realistic self-assessment, understanding, processing, purposeful action, difficulty, and so forth. These cognitively stimulating state descriptions are very important and valuable for both the learner and the teacher. Another advantage is that most of the procedures are quick to use, simple, and usually require little follow-up. What's more, tests steal time that is then lacking in actual learning.

A Dilemma Especially for Less Experienced Teachers

However, it should not be hidden that these collective feedbacks create a dilemma, especially for student teachers and less experienced teachers. It could be that the feedback requires adjustment in pace, procedure, level of difficulty, or ways of explaining. But that means more effort and more uncertainty because the teacher is not necessarily prepared for it and does not yet have the practices to adapt and rethink quickly. These teachers are therefore well advised to ask for such feedback when they have enough time to reflect on it afterward.

Don't Try to Be Loved (Students Prefer Authenticity to Ingratiation)

Teachers understandably want to know how they are perceived. The less experienced teachers in particular secretly want students to like them and to think they're a great teacher. But soliciting feedback in writing about the teacher's person and classroom management is tricky. The teacher must interpret and classify these feedbacks correctly, cope with critical judgments, and so forth. The danger is not small that flattering feedback is welcomed while negative statements tend to be averted or suppressed. The door is wide open for one-sided interpretations of this kind.

Therefore, this personal level should not necessarily be sought, just as—in the opposite direction—the teacher should also hold back with statements about the person of the student. So, the insight value is modest when students are asked to rate the quality of teaching and the manner of the teacher in a questionnaire. An anonymous mailbox in the classroom seems to be a simpler and more effective way for the students to express their discomfort, praise, and wishes.

SUMMATIVE ASSESSMENTS: ARE THE RESULTS AS EXPECTED?

The aim of summative assessments is to ascertain as reliably as possible what the students have learned. As shown in table 9.2, it must always be decided and transparently communicated what consequences the result of the summative assessment has, that is, whether further-reaching decisions are made on the basis of it (high-stakes grading) or not (low-stakes tests). Summative assessments can, but need not, be used for grading, promotion, and selection. For the time being, it is only a matter of systematically identifying learning achievement in a professional manner.

Grading Is Possible, but Not Mandatory

Thus, the teacher wants to find out as accurately as possible where everyone stands in comparison to the expected results that were initially set, no more and no less. However, unsatisfactory results do not necessarily lead to poor grades.

For example, in the face of poor results, a teacher may make an entirely different, actually more rational, decision: the teacher refrains from grading, and the points of the subject that are not understood are revisited, deepened, and practiced so that overall performance improves. In other words, the review process was strictly summative, but the teacher interprets the results formatively, giving students another chance to make progress.

Alleviating Emotional Pressure

Summative assessment of achievement is usually an emotionally charged affair; it is often associated with such diverse things as curiosity, frustration, relief, fear of failure, panic, parents' lack of understanding, conflicted discussions in the aftermath, discouragement, feelings of being overwhelmed.

It is therefore one of the most important educational achievements since around the turn of the millennium that attempts have been made to reform the rigid summative performance assessment, to expand the range of instruments, and to alleviate the emotional pressure.

FURTHER INFORMATION AND RESOURCES

TEST ANXIETY

One in Six Secondary School Students in England Is Highly Test Anxious

The following excerpt from a large British study provides some insight into the scope of text anxiety.

> The participants in this study were 2435 secondary school students. . . . In total, 16.4% of students reported themselves to be highly test anxious, with 22.5% of female students reporting themselves as highly test-anxious, compared to 10.3% of males. . . . [This] finding is, in itself, a cause for concern. Highly test anxious students tend to perform worse than their low test-anxious

counterparts, irrespective of their ability level, and test anxiety is related to a host of other variables that are indicative of disengagement from school or learning. (Putwain & Daly, 2014, pp. 564–565)

Reducing Test Anxiety While Increasing Learning: The Cheat Sheet

Here is a teacher's testimonial and a simple but quite original suggestion on how to reduce test anxiety and promote learning at the same time:

> Student learning is greatly enhanced by studying prior to an exam. Allowing students to prepare a cheat sheet for the exam helps structure this study time and deepens learning. The crib sheet is well defined: one double-sided page of notes. An award for the best and most creative cheat sheet allows the instructor to appreciate the students' efforts. Using the cheat sheet also reduces student anxiety during testing.
>
> . . . Students loved the idea of cheat sheets. They found, however, that they rarely needed them. Preparing the cheat sheets proved to be sufficient for learning what was on the test. This was the major difference between handing out information composed by me and having the students find their own. Students tailored the information to their own needs and wrote down information they still needed to learn. The act of writing and organizing the information for the cheat sheet allowed most students to fill in the holes in their knowledge. (Erbe, 2007, pp. 96–98)

Strictly Separate Formative and Summative Assessment

One tricky aspect is separating formative and summative assessment. Because formative assessment is carried out on an ongoing basis by teachers, there is a mistaken assumption "that all assessment by teachers is formative, adding to the blurring of the distinction between formative and summative purposes and to teachers changing their own on-going assessment into a series of 'mini' assessments each of which is essentially summative in character" (Harlen & James, 1997, p. 365).

The mixing of the two forms basically poisons students' learning; if they have to assume that everything goes into summative assessment, they no longer dare to make mistakes, and all learning becomes a kind of total testing situation. That's why it's so important that students know exactly: Now I'm not being assessed summatively; now I don't have to hide my shortcomings.

Increasing Variety of Expectations: More Demanding Assessments

Learners have been expected to produce a much greater variety of outcomes in recent years, and probably rightly so: pure knowledge and skill expectations are supplemented by broader and more complex goals. They focus, for example, on understanding, creativity, or communication skills, and they also include personal and interdisciplinary key competencies. The challenge for teachers is that they need to develop new procedures to reliably assess these areas.

For students, this means that it is often no longer enough to "know" something or to be able to perform a skill. With the requirements concerning the whole person—for example, their ability to cooperate, their commitment, their ability to organize themselves, their creativity—the assessment becomes more demanding, and the student, to a certain extent, a glass human being. This is not necessarily a bad thing, but it is important to realize that under these changed conditions, students are less able to hide; almost everything is assessed in some way.

Fairness: Assessment Perceived as Unfair Is a Disaster

Summative assessment is rarely an actual testing procedure that meets scientific criteria for quality, but the *principles of a fair assessment procedure* still fully apply, of course. Neglecting the fairness of assessment procedures creates great harm at all levels. Here are the most important principles:

Objectivity: No randomness

The procedure must not favor or disadvantage individual students and should eliminate randomness as much as possible.

Transparency: Everything is disclosed

Students must be informed about the procedure and whether it is a formative or summative assessment.

Reliability: Only the critical norm counts

The assessment criteria and procedures apply to all students, in other words, comparable performance is not arbitrarily assessed differently. This means that the criteria norm applies, which follows exclusively objective criteria and does not allow cross comparison with the class or longitudinal comparison with previous performance.

Validity: Only what is agreed upon is tested

The teacher's communicated intentions must also be clearly reflected in the criteria—meaning, only what was originally formulated as the goal is assessed.

Self-Assessment: Usually More Accurate Than You Think

A word about the integration of self-assessment: students are expected to account for their own learning and progress. We exclude here the case that students would assess their performance "tactically," that is, too well or too weakly, because they hope to gain an advantage.

Students are usually quite aware of where they stand and are good at assessing their performance, gaps, and potential. This is important for (self-)managing the learning process. However, if self-assessment is to be meaningfully included in summative assessment, there needs to be clear agreements with the students, clear procedures and criteria, and above all no mixing of formative and summative self-assessment.

It is bad for motivation if self-assessment and assessment by others diverge in the long run (cf., e.g., Hellmich & Günther, 2011). This increases the risk that the person concerned will give up and no longer see any point in making an effort. Ideally, therefore, the teacher and the student should reach a *consensual assessment*.

"EXAMS": A SPECIAL CASE

Written exams are a common but not unproblematic method of summative assessment. Criticisms of common assessment practices are numerous, and so is the literature on them. Here we can highlight only a few important points that are workable even for less experienced teachers.

Summative exams are not a very reliable measure of learning success because interests and emotions are focused less on the subject matter itself than on the assessment, and situational distortions are common despite or because of efforts to be objective. Exams are also quite time consuming; they tie up a lot of time in preparation, administration, measures to counteract writing off, and correction and debriefing—the latter is often ineffective because students' interest in the subject matter wanes and they are usually only interested in the results of the exam.

The following box, "Exams: If Anything, Then Fair, Reliable, Flexible, Anxiety-Free, and with Alternatives," presents the problem and shows numerous variations and alternatives to mitigate or overcome the unfavorable effects of exams.

EXAMS: IF ANYTHING, THEN FAIR, RELIABLE, FLEXIBLE, ANXIETY-FREE, AND WITH ALTERNATIVES

All experienced teachers have strong biographical experiences with summative, mostly written, performance assessment—all have experienced traditional testing with side effects in their own educational careers, especially in higher grades. This makes it all the more important not to adopt these practices unquestioningly. Reconsider the procedures and experiences and consider alternatives.

At the outset, graded summative assessments do not have to be tied to formal exams; many alternative forms have been established. But teachers do find themselves in a situation where they want to administer formal exams under strict conditions, the negative side effects should be eliminated as much as possible. The following sections deal only with this.

Absolutely Mandatory for a Fair Assessment in a Respectful Atmosphere

1. Climate

Liberate exams and tests from traditional, often frightening rituals. Avoid the following two pernicious things at all costs:
- It should be recalled once again: formative/supportive feedback must never mutate into summative assessments in retrospect.
- Summative assessments are not an instrument of classroom management. Do not give tests, oral quizzes, or graded homework without prior notice; do not use exams as punishment; do not use exams to establish silence.

Make every effort to maintain a friendly and focused, but not overly tense, atmosphere during exams and tests.

2. Clarity of intentions, content, and criteria

In advance of an exam (or other form of summative assessment, such as a test, a presentation, a lecture, a written paper) make all its terms transparent. Disclose the following:
- Your intentions and expectations: What do you want students to know, be able to do, show, and so on? Is it about reproducing factual knowledge? Is it about text comprehension? Is it about problem-solving strategies? Is it about error-free arithmetic? Is it about un-

derstanding connections? Is it about neat design? Is it about precise expression? The objectives must be clear enough to ensure that the students are not preparing for something that is not required. Usually, students can expect in exams what they have done in the activity phases and what was the subject of the previous tasks.

- The thematic content: Especially in written exams, it is important to specify the content area precisely. Vague statements are not enough (e.g., "in the textbook, pages 50 to 120" or "everything we have covered in the last five weeks").
- Grading criteria: How exactly will the performance be graded? What is important to the teacher, and how will it be graded (presentation, slips of the pen, time overruns, consequences for using unauthorized resources, etc.)?

3. Clarity of form and procedure (based on the test criterion "objectivity")

Announce to the students (1) how much time they have and what will happen if they finish before the time is up; (2) according to which formal guidelines they should write and hand in their work; and (3) what tools are allowed (smartphone, calculator, teaching aids, cheat sheets, prepared notes, etc.). You take the pressure off everyone if you allow as many aids as possible, which is unlikely to cause problems on understanding-based exams.

Give your students samples of exams or papers as you want them to be done. You can also give them an analogous, ungraded exam beforehand for practice purposes.

Individualized Testing Is Possible and Makes Sense

The final, unchangeable nature of an exam often seems so self-evident that it is no longer questioned. Does it have to be that way? No. Relentless testing has a very uncertain informative value and no educational value at all. If you want to prepare students for later exam situations, the best way is to teach them not to be afraid of exams.

Below are some variations on how you can move away from the "traditional" exam. At the same time, you will improve the quality and results of the assessment.

Variation 1: Voluntary retesting

You can have all students retake exams if they wish, at the end of the school day, for example. Of course, if students improve, the better grade applies. Voluntary retakes have several advantages:

- Students engage in better performance and learn as a result. What more could you ask for?
- Students learn that effort pays off, or to put it in technical terms: their self-efficacy beliefs improve, which has a positive impact on performance and motivation.
- Student (and parent) satisfaction improves, and testing procedures are perceived as more equitable.

You may have concerns. Here are the counterarguments to possible objections:

- Contrary to possible fears, the effort is limited: It is easy for you to vary an existing exam with little effort. In the case of self-written papers, you just give the student the opportunity to revise.
- You have little additional time burden if the retest is moved to free time; while the student is working, you are engaged in other activities.
- If someone objects that retakes create a practice effect, which actually makes the exam increasingly easier, then counter: that is the best thing that can happen!

Variation 2: Time-shifted summative assessments as an alternative

When is the best time for summative review? A low score for something you're good at a few days after the exam is unfair. Why not assess the skill when the student is ready?

Therein lies a fundamental problem with all exams. The solution is as simple as it takes some getting used to: *students choose the time of the exams themselves.* You can implement it without any problems:

- You offer several dates, and students choose the date of their choice.
- You have a larger set of tasks that are suitable for the exam, including the tasks that students have already worked on in an activity phase, with minor modifications at best. When students feel ready, they report and take their exam. This can easily be done in class, for example, during seatwork.

Variation 3: Different requirements in terms of content

Students perform at different levels. This is reflected in the summative assessment because it is based on the criteria norm and no longer takes into account the particular circumstances of the individual students or the class. As a result, the gap widens, and low-performing students are graded lower. This has a negative impact on motivation, self-concept, and overall performance.

If weaker students cannot achieve adequate grades with sufficient effort, something has gone wrong. All students should achieve the basic requirements of the class, which is why they are called "basic."

What does this mean for exams? Determine what basic requirements all students can achieve with reasonable effort; give a passing grade for that. Then tell students: "I know everyone has mastered these basic things. Okay, if you solve this basic part of the test, the grade will be sufficient."

For example, in a math exam, students know which basic tasks will get them a sufficient grade; anything above that will raise the grade to the highest possible.

Variation 4: Include self-assessment

If you always make the goals, tasks, and success criteria transparent, as has been emphasized throughout this book, students will learn over time to accurately self-assess; after all, they are constantly learning about the extent to which their performance deviates from the success criteria, which in turn promotes learning and achievement (Andrade & Valtcheva, 2009). You can take advantage of this for exams as well.

Student self-assessments are not a substitute for summative assessments by the teacher or by tests, and yet they are important: significant discrepancies in peer and self-assessment are a kind of seismograph for inconsistencies, whether in the assessment itself or in the circumstances that do not allow students to demonstrate their knowledge and skills. You are therefore well advised to ask students to self-assess at the same time as they take the test.

In practice, you can proceed like this:
- Before the exam, students write down on the exam sheet the expected grade that they think corresponds to their ability.
- After the exam, students note on the exam sheet the grade they probably achieved and a comment on it.
- Subsequently, you write the grade actually achieved next to it.

If the three grades are significantly different, or if the comment reveals a serious problem, talk to the student and try to figure out what the reason might be and what to do now.

How to Further Improve the Quality and Fairness of Summative Procedures

Expand your repertoire and latitude in forms and procedures of summative assessments:

Beyond exams: Alternatives to written exams and tests

Many alternatives to written tests have been developed in recent years, such as the assessment of written work and portfolios; the evaluation of individual, partner, and group work in class; or observation according to specific criteria—even abandoning formal tests altogether, as is often the case in physical education, for example.

Also ask more open questions and problems

Because they are easier to review, exams tend to ask straightforward questions—they focus on the recall of factual and skill knowledge. More open-ended questions and problems, on the other hand, allow students to better express their understanding, ideas, and insights.

Always use the criteria norm, don't manipulate the average

Summative assessments are always based on the criteria norm, there is no way around this. Thus, the assessment criteria are fact bound and not dependent on class average or other influencing factors. In concrete terms, this means that it is clear from the outset which performance will be assessed and how, or how the grade will be arrived at. If overall performance is above expectations, so much the better. If it is below expectations, you need to get to the bottom of the causes and, for those who wish to do so, consider retaking the exam (see variation 1 above). Completely unacceptable is the practice of manipulating the average after the fact by changing the scale.

Don't get involved in mathematical games with grade—
grades should be fair, that's all

Let's take a few questions as an example:
- Should exam papers not turned in be counted as a zero or not?
- What to do if students are always absent on exam days?
- What grade do I give if I catch a student cheating?

There is always a formalistic answer to these, which is almost always unfair. Or you can respond smoothly and try to find out what the student's capacity really is despite the unfavorable circumstances (which is what assessment is all about).

In all three cases above, it would be completely unfair to give a zero, because a final grade must reflect the student's capacity as accurately as possible, even if you don't like students cheating or being opportunistic. Therefore, another way of arriving at an appropriate grade must be found.

Epilogue

What Is the Plan?

To plan means to have a plan, a strategy: The coach has a plan to win the game. The advertiser has a plan to attract new customers. The conductor has a plan to make the orchestra sound its best. The engineer has a plan for the perfect product.

And what is the plan of the teacher? We know, it's about the students, and only the students: that they make progress, that they achieve, experience success, cooperate, get help when needed, feel understood, but also: that they are taken out of their comfort zone, challenged, confronted with new things, shown how to resolve conflict situations, taught how to deal with frustrations.

Yet sometimes the central plan gets lost from view. Teachers and student teachers deal with many other things around this core of being a teacher. At best, those subsidiary activities are there to implement the central plan. They are mostly well intentioned and intended to move teachers forward and help them, which is especially the case in teacher education. But they tend to gradually overshadow the real purpose, and over time some teachers get the feeling that their job consists mainly of working through all these more peripheral things.

So sometimes the side issues become the main issue: filling out lesson plan templates, delivering lessons, taking a test, doing all the paperwork, dealing with classroom management, and during teacher education, handling all the tasks associated with training on top of that.

The intent of this book on planning is to put things in their place and distinguish between the end and the means to the end. From the end, that is, from the benefit to student progress, it is easier to see what really contributes to the good, lean, and effective plan and what contributes less, that is, to distinguish the important from the redundant and to repriori-tize. Such careful readjustment frees up energies that can be used more purposefully.

References

Anderson, L. W., & Krathwohl, D. R. (Eds.) (2001). *A taxonomy for learning, teaching, and assessing: A revision of Bloom's taxonomy of educational objectives.* Addison Wesley Longman.

Andersson, H., Jönsson, H., & Axäter, S. (1980). A simulation study of hierarchical production-inventory control. *OR Spectrum, 2,* 79–89.

Andrade, H., & Valtcheva, A. (2009). Promoting learning and achievement through self-assessment. *Theory into Practice, 48*(1), 12–19.

Angelo, T. A., & Cross, K. P. (1993). *Classroom assessment techniques: a handbook for college teachers* (2nd ed.). San Francisco: Jossey-Bass.

Ball, D. L., & Forzani, F. M. (2009). The work of teaching and the challenge for teacher education. *Journal of Teacher Education, 60*(5), 497–511.

Berg, C., & Clough, M. P. (1991). Hunter lesson design: The wrong one for science teaching. *Educational Leadership, 46*(4).

Berliner, D. C. (2001). Learning about and learning from expert teachers. *International Journal of Educational Research, 35*(5), 463–482.

Biggs, J., & Collis, K. (1982). *Evaluating the quality of learning: The SOLO taxonomy.* Academic Press.

Black, P. (2015). Formative assessment: An optimistic but incomplete vision. *Assessment in Education: Principles, Policy & Practice, 22*(1), 161–177.

Bloom, B. S., Engelhart, M. D., Furst, E. J., Hill, W. H., & Krathwohl, D. R. (1956). *Taxonomy of educational objectives. Handbook I: Cognitive domain.* McKay.

Blum, W., Krauss, S., & Neubrand, M. (2011). COACTIV – Ein mathematikdidaktisches Projekt? In M. Kunter, J. Baumert, W. Blum, U. Klusmann, S. Krauss, & M. Neubrand (Eds.), *Professionelle Kompetenz von Lehrkräften: Ergebnisse des Forschungsprogramms COACTIV* (pp. 329–343). Münster: Waxmann.

Borko, H., & Livingston, C. (1989). Cognition and improvisation: Differences in mathematics instruction by expert and novice teachers. *American Educational Research Journal, 26,* 473–498.

Bowers, L. V. (1971). *Lessons Learned*. San Francisco: Department of the Army.

Causton-Theoharis, J. N., Theoharis, G. T., & Trezek, B. J. (2008). Teaching pre-service teachers to design inclusive instruction: A lesson planning template. *International Journal of Inclusive Education, 12*(4), 381–399.

CCSSO. (2010). *Common Core State Standards for English Language Arts & Literacy in History/Social Studies, Science, and Technical Subjects*. Washington: Council of Chief State School Officers.

Compayré, G. (1908). *Herbart and education by instruction*. London: George G. Harrap.

Dodd, C. I. (1898). *Introduction to the Herbartian Principles of Teaching*. New York: Macmillan.

Dolin, J., Black, P., Harlen, W., & Tiberghien, A. (2017). Exploring relations between formative and summative assessment. In J. Dolin & R. Evans (Eds.), *Transforming assessment through an interplay between practice, research and policy* (pp. 53–80). Springer.

Doran, G. T. (1981). There's a S.M.A.R.T. way to write management's goals and objectives. *Management Review, 70*(11), 35–36.

Drost, B. R., & Levine, A. C. (2015). An analysis of strategies for teaching standards-based lesson plan alignment to preservice teachers. *Journal of Education, 195*(2), 37–47.

Erbe, B. (2007). Reducing test anxiety while increasing learning: The cheat sheet. *College Teaching, 55*(3), 96–98.

Fraefel, U. (2023). *Core practices of successful teachers: Supporting learning and managing instruction*. Maryland: Rowman & Littlefield.

Friesen, N. (2010). Lesson planning: Anglo-American perspectives. *Bildung und Erziehung, 63*(4), 417–430.

Gagné, R. M. (1974). *Essentials of learning for instruction*. Dryden.

Gagné, R. M., Briggs, L. J., & Wager, W. W. (1992). *Principles of instructional design* (4th ed.; 1st ed. 1974). Holt, Rinehart and Winston.

Gamson, D. A., Eckert, S. A., & Anderson, J. (2019). Standards, instructional objectives and curriculum design: A complex relationship. *Phi Delta Kappan, 100*(6), 8–12.

Grossman, P. (Ed.) (2018). *Teaching core practices in teacher education*. Harvard Education Press.

Grossman, P., Hammerness, K., & McDonald, M. (2009). Redefining teaching, re-imagining teacher education. *Teachers and Teaching: Theory and Practice, 15*(2), 273–289.

Guise, M., Habib, M., Thiessen, K., & Robbins, A. (2017). Continuum of co-teaching implementation: Moving from traditional student teaching to co-teaching. *Teaching & Teacher Education, 66*, 370–382.

Harlen, W., & James, M. (1997). Assessment and learning: differences and relationships between formative and summative assessment. *Assessment in Education: Principles, Policy & Practice, 4*(3), 365–379.

Hatch, L., & Clark, S. K. (2021). A study of the instructional decisions and lesson planning strategies of highly effective rural elementary school teachers. *Teaching and Teacher Education, 108*.

Hellmich, F., & Günther, F. (2011). Entwicklung von Selbstkonzepten bei Kindern im Grundschulalter: Ein Überblick. In F. Hellmich (Ed.), *Selbstkonzepte im*

Grundschulalter: Modelle, empirische Ergebnisse, pädagogische Konsequenzen (S. 17–46). Kohlhammer.

Hume, A., Cooper, R., & Borowski, A. (Eds.). (2019). *Repositioning pedagogical content knowledge in teachers' knowledge for teaching science.* Springer.

Hunter, M. (1976). Teacher competency: Problem, theory, and practice. *Theory into Practice, 15*(2), 162–171.

Hunter, M. (1994). *Enhancing teaching.* Macmillan.

John, P. D. (2006). Lesson planning and the student teacher: Re-thinking the dominant model. *Curriculum Studies, 38*(4), 483–498.

Jones, K. A., Jones, J., & Vermette, P. J. (2011). Six common lesson planning pitfalls: Recommendations for novice educators. *Education, 131*(4), 845–864.

Kagan, D. M. (1992). Professional growth among preservice and beginning teachers. *Review of Educational Research, 62*(2), 129–169.

König, J., Buchholtz, C., & Dohmen, D. (2015). Analyse von schriftlichen Unterrichtsplanungen: Empirische Befunde zur didaktischen Adaptivität als Aspekt der Planungskompetenz angehender Lehrkräfte. *Zeitschrift für Erziehungswissenschaft, 18*, 375–404.

Mager, R. F. (1962). *Preparing instructional objectives.* Palo Alto.

McConnell, C., Conrad, B. M., & Uhrmacher, B. P. (2020). *Lesson planning with purpose: Five approaches to curriculum design.* Teachers College Press.

McDonald, J. P. (1992). Dilemmas of planning backwards: Rescuing a good idea. *Teachers College Record, 94*(1), 152–169.

McTighe, J., Doubet, K., & Carbaugh, E. M. (2020). *Designing authentic performance tasks and projects: Tools for meaningful learning and assessment.* ASCD.

Munthe, E., & Conway, P. F. (2017). Evolution of research on teachers' planning: Implications for teacher education. In D. J. Clandinin & J. Husu (Eds.), *SAGE handbook of research on teacher education.* Sage.

Murphy, C., & Scantlebury, K. (Eds.). (2010). *Coteaching in international contexts: Research and practice.* Springer.

Oelkers, J. (2009). Lehrerbildung an der Pädagogischen Hochschule zwischen Wissenschaft, Politik und Gesellschaft. *Festvortrag anlässlich des Hochschultages der Pädagogischen Hochschule Weingarten am 20. November 2009.*

Orlich, D. C., Harder, R. J., Callahan, R. C., Trevisan, M. S., & Brown, A. H. (2004). *Teaching strategies: A guide to effective instruction* (7th ed.). Houghton Mifflin.

Ornstein, A. C. (1997). How teachers plan lessons. *High School Journal, 80*(4), 227–237.

Ornstein, A. C., & Lasley, T. J. I. (2000). *Strategies of effective teaching* (3rd ed.). McGraw Hill.

Oser, F. K., & Baeriswyl, F. J. (2001). Choreographies of teaching: Bridging instruction to learning. In V. Richardson (Ed.), *AERA's handbook of research on teaching* (pp. 1031–1065). American Educational Research Association.

Putwain, D., & Daly, A. L. (2014). Test anxiety prevalence and gender differences in a sample of English secondary school students. *Educational Studies, 40*(5), 554–570.

Rabin, C. (2020). Co-teaching: Collaborative and caring teacher preparation. *Journal of Teacher Education, 71*(1), 135–147.

Rose, E. D. (1962). Screen writing and the delicate art of persuasion. *Journal of the University Film Producers Association, 14*(2), 8–10, 23.

Sánchez, G., & Valcárcel, M. V. (1999). Science teachers' views and practices in planning for teaching. *Journal of Research in Science Teaching, 36*(4), 493–513.

Sawyer, R. K. (2004). Creative teaching: Collaborative discussion as disciplined improvisation. *Educational Researcher, 33*(2), 12–20.

Seel, A. (1997). Von der Unterrichtsplanung zum konkreten Lehrerhandeln: Eine Untersuchung zum Zusammenhang von Planung und Durchführung von Unterricht bei Hauptschullehrerstudentinnen. *Unterrichtswissenschaft, 25*(3), 257–273.

Shavelson, J. R. (1987). Planning. In M. Dunkin (Ed.), *International encyclopedia of teaching and teacher education* (pp. 483–486). Pergamon.

Shulman, L. S. (1986). Those who understand: Knowledge growth in teaching. *Educational Researcher, 15*(2), 4–14.

Stronge, J. H., & Xu, X. (2016). *Instructional planning for effective teaching.* Solution Tree Press.

TeachingWorks (n.d.). *High-Leverage Practices.* TeachingWorks Resource Library. Retrieved April 17, 2023, from https://library.teachingworks.org/curriculum-resources/high-leverage-practices/.

Tyler, R. W. (1949). *Basic principles of curriculum and instruction.* University of Chicago Press.

Uhrmacher, B. P., Conrad, B. M., & Moroye, C. M. (2013). Finding the balance between process and product through perceptual lesson planning. *Teachers College Record, 115*(7), 1–27.

Vermette, P. J., Jones, K. A., Jones, J. L., Werner, T., Kline, C., & D'Angelo, J. (2010). A model for planning learning experiences to promote achievement in diverse secondary classrooms. *SRATE Journal, 19*(2), 70–83.

Werner, J., Wernke, S., & Zierer, K. (2017). In S. Wernke & K. Zierer (Eds.), *Die Unterrichtsplanung: Ein in Vergessenheit geratener Kompetenzbereich?! Status Quo und Perspektiven aus Sicht der empirischen Forschung* (S. 104–120). Klinkhardt.

Wernke, S., & Zierer, K. (Eds.) (2017). *Die Unterrichtsplanung: Ein in Vergessenheit geratener Kompetenzbereich?! Status Quo und Perspektiven aus Sicht der empirischen Forschung.* Klinkhardt.

West, L., & Staub, F. C. (2003). *Content-focused coaching: Transforming mathematics lessons.* Heinemann.

Wiggins, G., & McTighe, J. (1998). *Understanding by design.* ASCD.

Wiggins, G., & McTighe, J. (2006). *Understanding by design* (2nd ed.). Pearson Merrill Prentice Hall.

Wiggins, G., & McTighe, J. (2011). *The understanding by design guide to creating high-quality units.* ASCD.

Windschitl, M., Thompson, J., Braaten, M., & Stroupe, D. (2012). Proposing a core set of instructional practices and tools for teachers of science. *Science Education, 96*(5), 878–903.

Womack, S. T., Pepper, S., Hanna, S. L., & Bell, C. D. (2015). *Most effective practices in lesson planning.* Retrieved from ERIC: http://files.eric.ed.gov/fulltext/ED553616.pdf.

Yinger, R. J. (1980). A study of teacher planning. *Elementary School Journal, 80*(3), 107–127.

Zahorik, J. A. (1975). Teachers' planning models. *Educational Leadership, 33*(2), 134–139.

About the Author

Urban Fraefel is professor emeritus of the School of Education at the University of Applied Sciences and Arts of Northwestern Switzerland, where he established and coordinated the structures and research activities of studies on professional practice. Moreover, he has held the position of director of the Institute of Secondary Education. Previously, he was in charge of the teaching and learning of science at the secondary level at the University of Zurich and a member of the founding council of the School of Education Zurich, responsible for the development of field experiences and for the division of educational psychology. Beyond that, Urban Fraefel has a broad experience as a teacher on all levels.

In recent years, Urban Fraefel's research focuses on practice-based education of student teachers in collaboration between universities and schools, assessment of competencies in professional practice, and core practices of teaching especially in initial teacher education. In addition to numerous publications in these fields, he is also a textbook author. Urban Fraefel is furthermore the founder and honorary president of the International Society for Studies on Professional Practice and Professionalization (IGSP).